# Leckie
the education publisher
## for Scotland

KU-360-217

# National 5
# FRENCH

For SQA 2019 and beyond

## Revision + Practice
## 2 Books in 1

© 2020 Leckie

001/15102020

10 9 8 7 6 5 4 3 2 1

All rights reserved. No part of this publication may be reproduced,
stored in a retrieval system, or transmitted in any form or by any
means, electronic, mechanical, photocopying, recording or
otherwise, without the prior written permission of the Publisher or
a licence permitting restricted copying in the United Kingdom
issued by the Copyright Licensing Agency Ltd., 90 Tottenham
Court Road, London W1T 4LP.

ISBN 9780008435370

*Published by*
Leckie
An imprint of HarperCollinsPublishers
Westerhill Road, Bishopbriggs, Glasgow, G64 2QT
T: 0844 576 8126     F: 0844 576 8131
leckiescotland@harpercollins.co.uk     www.leckiescotland.co.uk

Publisher: Sarah Mitchell
Project Managers: Harley Griffiths and Lauren Murray

*Special thanks to*
QBS (layout and illustration)

Printed and bound in Great Britain by
CPI Group (UK) Ltd, Croydon, CR0 4YY

A CIP Catalogue record for this book is available from the
British Library.

*Acknowledgements*
P93 © 360b / Shutterstock.com

All other images © Shutterstock.com

Whilst every effort has been made to trace the copyright holders,
in cases where this has been unsuccessful, or if any have
inadvertently been overlooked, the Publishers would gladly
receive any information enabling them to rectify any error or
omission at the first opportunity.

**ebook**

To access the ebook version of this Revision Guide visit
www.collins.co.uk/ebooks
and follow the step-by-step instructions.

# Introduction

# Part 1: Revision guide

## Society

## Learning and employability

# Contents

ANSWERS Check your answers to the practice test papers online:
www.collins.co.uk/pages/Scottish-curriculum-free-resources

# Introduction

## Complete Revision and Practice

This Complete **two-in-one Revision and Practice** book is designed to support you as students of National 5 French. It can be used either in the classroom, for regular study and homework, or for exam revision. By combining **a revision guide and two full sets of practice test papers**, this book includes everything you need to be fully familiar with the National 5 French exam. As well as including ALL the core course content with practice opportunities, there is comprehensive assignment and exam preparation advice with revision question and practice test paper answers provided online at www.collins.co.uk/pages/Scottish-curriculum-free-resources

## About the revision guide

The revision guide is grouped into each of the topic areas and includes vocabulary, easy to follow grammar guides, and listening, reading and writing exercises in each section. This should help you to ensure that you've covered everything you need to feel ready for your final assessments.

In addition to this, there are sections at the end of this revision guide designed to give you extra support in preparing for your talking, writing, reading and listening assessments. There is also a key vocabulary section that includes a bank of high-frequency vocabulary, the top verbs you should be familiar with for National 5 (the most common words that come up all the time), some other basic vocabulary (numbers, etc.) and, of course, lots of exercises and top tips to help you remember it all!

**Audio tracks to support all listening activities in this book are available to download from the Leckie website. Go to https://collins.co.uk/pages/scottish-curriculum-free-resources-french**

## About the practice papers

The practice paper section contains two Reading, two Writing and two Listening practice test papers which mirror the actual SQA exams as much as possible. The layout and question level are all similar to the exams that you will sit, so that you are familiar with what they will look like.

Audio tracks to accompany the listening exams can be downloaded, free, from the Leckie & Leckie website at https://collins.co.uk/pages/scottish-curriculum-free-resources-french

The practice papers can be used in two ways:

1. You can complete an entire practice paper under exam-style conditions by setting yourself a time for each paper and answering it as well as possible without using any notes.
2. You can answer the practice paper questions as a revision exercise, using your notes to produce model answers.

Both practice papers in this book have answers to the Reading and Listening papers provided online at www.collins.co.uk/pages/Scottish-curriculum-free-resources so that you can see what is expected for each question. There are also 'Hints' for each answer, which explain the answers in more detail. This is to help you understand where the answers are found in the Reading and Listening passages and what each question is testing. Look at these carefully as they will help you to understand what is expected of you when you sit your exam.

# Course summary

To start with, let's look at how the course is structured. Getting this clear in your head before you begin to study is an important part of your preparation. It will help you plan your revision and make sure you are clear about what you need to know right from the start.

The National 5 course has been designed to support you in developing French language skills in **reading**, **listening**, **talking** and **writing** in four different contexts: **society, learning, employability** and **culture**.

Within each of these contexts there are different topics, and within each of the topics there are suggested areas for topic development. The topic development really just means the vocabulary areas that you will cover as part of these topics.

The table below gives you an overview of the contexts, the topics and the topic development of the National 5 course.

| Context | Topics | Topic development |
|---|---|---|
| **Society** | Family and friends | Family and friends |
| | | Relationships |
| | | Ideal parents |
| | | Types of friends |
| | | Peer pressure |
| | Lifestyles | Health and wellbeing |
| | | Lifestyle-related illnesses |
| | | Advantages/disadvantages of a healthy/unhealthy lifestyle |
| | Media | Reality TV |
| | | Advantages/disadvantages of new technology, e.g. Internet, mobile phones |
| | Global languages | Language learning and relevance |
| | Citizenship | Description of local area as a tourist centre |
| | | Comparison of town and country life |
| | | Being environmentally friendly in the home |
| **Learning** | Learning in context | Activities you like and dislike in modern languages and other subjects |
| | | Preparing for exams |
| | Education | Comparing education systems |
| | | Improving your own education system |
| | | Learner responsibilities |
| **Employability** | Jobs | Part-time jobs and studying |
| | | Qualities for present/future jobs |
| | | Future plans |
| | Work and CVs | Planning and reporting back on work experience |
| | | Reviewing achievements and ambitions |

| Context | Topics | Topic development |
|---------|--------|-------------------|
| Culture | Planning a trip | Importance of travel and learning a foreign language |
| | | Describing your best holiday |
| | | Attitudes to travel |
| | Other countries | Aspects of other countries including educational, political, social and economic aspects |
| | Celebrating a special event | Comparing special events, traditions, celebrations and events in another country |
| | | Importance of customs and traditions |
| | Literature of another country | Literary fiction, e.g. short stories – understanding and analysing |
| | Film and television | Studying films in modern languages |
| | | Studying television in other countries |

All of your National 5 assessments will link to these contexts and topic areas, so it's important that you cover them as part of your revision.

## Assessment summary

There are two parts to National 5 assessment:

### 1. Writing assignment

National 5 French includes a writing assignment as part of your overall assessment. This is prepared as part of coursework in class, completed as a final draft under assessment conditions and then externally assessed by the SQA. You will have a chance to draft, redraft and make corrections before you create your final folio. The marks you gain for this will contribute towards your overall award and it is a great opportunity to develop your writing skills and really show what you can do. Make sure this is your best work and challenge yourself to produce the most interesting and accurate language you can. It's a great chance to get some extra marks in the bank, so use it to your advantage!

### 2. External assessments

The external assessments are your final exams. These are graded A–D and this grade is determined by a percentage of your overall marks for each of the assessments listed below.

The percentages are usually as follows:

A   **70% and above**

B   **60%**

C   **50%**

D   **40%**

**TOP TIP**

Be well prepared for your talking and writing assessments so that you can pick up as many marks as possible. These are two areas you can prepare for in advance and learn a lot of prior to the assessment. Always remember that an extra half hour of practice could be the difference between an A and a B!

This percentage is taken as a mark out of 120 from the following assessments combined:

| Assessment | Breakdown | Marks | Total marks |
|---|---|---|---|
| Performance (listening and talking) | Presentation | 10 | 30 |
| | Discussion | 15 | |
| | Natural spontaneous conversation | 5 | |
| Reading and writing | Reading | 30 | 50 |
| | Writing | 20 | |
| Listening | Listening | 20 | 20 |
| Assignment | Writing | 20 | 20 |
| **Total marks** | | | 120 |

# Assessment in detail

## Performance (listening and talking)

Your performance assessment is a test of your ability to talk, listen and respond in the language. There are **two** main parts to this assessment: a **presentation** and then a **follow-up discussion**. You can choose which context you would like to present on and discuss, and this could be from any one of society, learning, employability or culture.

**Exam time:** Approximately 6–8 minutes in total (1–2 minutes of presentation with 5–6 minutes of follow-up discussion).

**Presentation:** 10 marks
**Discussion:** 15 marks
**Natural spontaneous conversation:** 5 marks

**Total performance marks:** 30
**Percentage of overall mark:** 25

Your choice of topic is important and it is worth choosing something you feel comfortable with and happy to talk about. If you love sports, for example, choose to talk about them. It's always easier to talk about something you enjoy!

The presentation should last approximately **1–2 minutes**. As it can be prepared by you in advance, this is really a chance for you to shine and show what you can do in French. You are allowed five headings, of not more than eight words per heading, which you can use as an aide-memoire during the assessment. These can be in French or in English. Learn your presentation as well as you can in advance and you will benefit from feeling more relaxed and comfortable on the day of the assessment.

Your teacher will most likely make a comment about how interesting your presentation was and then will go on to ask you questions related to the topic. This is the start of the conversation part of the assessment.

The conversation will last approximately **5–6 minutes** and you will be marked on various different elements, e.g. your accuracy and ability to communicate clearly when speaking French, your ability to understand the questions, how well you can maintain a conversation and how natural you sound. Your conversation should cover at least 2 different contexts, e.g. school and family life. You can only ever get a maximum of 9/15 if you only cover one theme, so make sure there is variety and that you are prepared to talk about different things!

You can prepare for the conversation if you know roughly the types of things you might be asked about. For example, if you are presenting about your pastimes and sport then you might be asked about healthy living more generally. You can look at the context you have chosen and make sure you have lots of answers prepared for this. You can't have all the answers prepared off by heart, but it helps to have a bank of good phrases you can use to help your conversation to stand out.

## TOP TIPS FOR TALKING

- Talking can be really nerve-racking and a lot of students become anxious about this part of the assessment. Be as prepared as you can be to help calm your nerves and imagine yourself in the exam situation speaking French really well and being relaxed and confident. Think of yourself as being successful and you will do better as a result.

- Have a rescue phrase ready in case you don't know what to say or have a long hesitation. Hesitation is normal and natural – it's how you recover that is the main thing. A generic phrase like, 'I'm not sure what I think about that, it's all the same to me' or 'Sorry, I lost my train of thought' can rescue you from a long pause when you've gone completely blank.

- Record yourself or ask your teacher/foreign language assistant to record themselves reading your presentation and listen to it all the time to help you remember it off by heart. Other than that, you just have to practise, practise and practise some more until it's perfect.

## Reading and writing exam

Your reading and writing exams are grouped together and there is no break between starting one paper and then moving on to the next. Be aware of this and practise getting your timings right to make sure you leave yourself enough time for both. Most people would probably need about an hour for the reading and then 30 minutes for the writing.

**Exam time:** 1 hour 30 minutes
**Reading:** 30 marks
**Writing:** 20 marks

**Total paper marks:** 50
**Percentage of overall mark:** 37.5

## Reading

The reading is made up of **three texts** (each worth 10 marks) and accompanying comprehension questions. Each question is worth a different number of marks and you should use this as a guide to how much information you should write for each answer. Make sure you include all details, as these are usually required in order to get even just 1 mark.

There is also one question known as the 'overall purpose question'. It is designed to see if you have understood the purpose of a reading text as a whole and will usually be a tick-box question, so you will be able to choose the answer.

You are allowed to use a dictionary in this exam.

## TOP TIPS FOR READING

- Always read the questions carefully before you read the text. This will give you a good understanding of the text before you start and will give you an idea of what you are looking for in your answers.

- Always answer in full sentences. This helps ensure that you give enough detail. A lot of marks are lost just through missing out key details. For example, answering 'By the beach' as opposed to 'Their summer house is located by a small beach'.

- Make sure your answers make sense and the English is correct. This can often be the biggest mistake candidates make, and can lose you marks.

- Never miss out the extra information. Words like 'very', 'often', 'a little', 'a lot' are often required to get you 1 mark so make sure you include them in your answers where they come up in the text. For example, 'She eats ice-cream' will get you no marks, but 'She eats a lot of ice-cream' will get you 1 mark.

## Writing

The context for the writing part of the exam is a job application for which you will have to write between **120 and 150** words in French. You are allowed a dictionary in this exam.

You won't know what the job is but you can prepare text that can then be adapted, such as:

To whom it may concern, My name is _____. I'm a student in _____ and I am looking for work experience in France. I would therefore like to apply for the job of _____.

There are six bullet points in total which then have to be answered in your job application. Four of these are always the same, so you can prepare these in advance:

- Personal details (name, age, where you live)
- School/college/education experience until now
- Skills/interests you have which make you right for the job
- Related work experience

You should write **20–30 words** for each of these bullet points.

The last two bullet points are unseen in advance but they will relate to the world of work, e.g. when you are available to start work, if you have any experience of using your language skills in the workplace, if you have experience of working with the public, etc. This means that, up to a point, you can prepare these too. The writing section at the back of the revision guide has a bank of vocabulary that you can use to help you prepare for this section of the writing paper.

You should write **at least 15 words** for the final two unseen bullet points.

## TOP TIPS FOR WRITING

- You can learn a lot of the writing task beforehand and be as prepared as you can in advance for this exam. See this as a gift. Being prepared will help you feel more relaxed about it, and having a good piece of writing ready will ensure you can pick up extra marks easily.

- Choose to include some complicated and interesting phrases – this will make your writing stand out.

- Use a variety of verbs and tenses to demonstrate your knowledge of the language.

## Listening

**Exam time:** 25 minutes
**Total marks:** 20
**Percentage of overall mark:** 25

There are two parts to the listening exam. In the first part, you will listen to a monologue (one person talking) and answer comprehension questions, plus one overall purpose question about what they have said. These questions will be worth 8 marks in total. You will hear the monologue three times, with a pause of 1 minute between each playing.

In the second part, you will listen to a conversation between two people. This will often be in the form of an interview. As in the first part, you will listen to the conversation three times altogether, with a pause of 1 minute between each playing. The questions for this part of the assessment are all comprehension questions and are worth a total of 12 marks.

All questions are in English.

## TOP TIPS FOR LISTENING

- It is crucial that you read the questions carefully before you start a listening assessment. Pick out the key words from each question so that you know for what you are listening out. For example, if the question is 'What did he like about the job?', then listen for positive things said about work. Have a quick think in advance about what these things could be. This will help you identify the answers as they come up. Circling question words like when and where can help to focus your attention on the key details to listen out for.

- Take notes and answer the questions in sentences during the pauses. Listening and writing simultaneously is a skill, so practise doing this in note form as you listen. When you have the 1-minute pause, you will then be able to return to the text and write out your answers in full (including all details of course!)

- Have a listening assessment routine. Know exactly how you are going to use your time in the listening and apply it whenever you revise or complete practice papers. This might include reading the questions, quickly mind mapping possible answers, taking notes when listening, and writing your answers in the pauses. Having a method and an approach helps to build confidence.

- Predicting possible answers can help you think of possible vocabulary which might come up.

## Assignment – Writing

The writing assignment gives you an opportunity to develop your writing skills in class and to gain extra valuable marks! It is worth 20 marks altogether and should be between 120–200 words in length. Your teacher will give you a scenario in English which you will then respond to. This could cover any of the themes of Society, Learning or Culture. The essay is then written in class, marked by your teacher with a marking code which highlights the points which need to be corrected. You will have a chance to redraft it and to create a final version which will be submitted to the SQA. The SQA will then mark the assignment out of 20 as part of your overall award. Make sure you are happy with your final copy before you submit it! Don't have any marks or comments on it and make sure it is clear and tidy – this won't necessarily help with your marks, but it is always better to produce well-presented work which you can be proud of!

> **Exam time:** In class with time for several drafts and redrafts
> **Total marks:** 20
>
> **Percentage of overall mark:** 12.5

When you are writing your essay, the kinds of supports you can use are:

- The assignment question in English
- Grammar reference notes, e.g. verb tables or notes on forming the perfect/imperfect tense
- Bilingual dictionary
- Wordlist or vocabulary list
- Writing improvement codes or notes
- Draft versions or notes

You cannot use materials such as text books, online resources, lists of phrases or jotters. This is all designed to help you to develop the skills to write independently and to think critically. It can be challenging to write accurately and confidently in another language, so use your notes and knowledge to stretch yourself in a structured way.

When answering the questions, you don't need to answer all the bullet points but be aware that the scenario probably will give you a natural essay structure.

The assignment is another gift and a great chance to show what you can do and gain marks! Use it to your advantage. *Bon courage et bonne chance*!

### TOP TIPS FOR THE WRITING ASSIGNMENT

Some key things to think of when you are writing might be:

- Introduction, 3 × paragraphs – each 2 sentences long, conclusion.
- Include your opinions, e.g. *à mon avis, je pense que, en ce qui me concerne*, etc.
- Vary your sentence length and use connectors, e.g. *mais, et, parce que, car*, etc.
- Check for gender (*un, une, des, le, la, les*), verb, tense, plurals, spelling.
- Focus on accuracy.
- Add some star dust! Add some fantastic French which will make your writing shine!

# National 5
# FRENCH

For SQA 2019 and beyond

## Revision Guide

Ann Robertson

# Family

As you move into National 5 level, family and friends vocabulary develops and now focuses on your relationships. Be proud of this progression in your French knowledge and always be sure to show off what you can do.

## Vocabulary: family relationships

Let's look at describing relationships within your family.

| | |
|---|---|
| *Nous (ne) sommes (pas) une famille unie* | We are (not) a close family |
| *Je m'entends très bien avec* | I get on really well with |
| *Je ne m'entends pas bien avec* | I don't get on well with |
| *J'aime passer du temps avec ma famille* | I like spending time with my family |
| *On se dispute souvent* | We often argue |
| *On ne se dispute jamais* | We never argue |
| *On se dispute à propos de l'argent* | We argue about money |
| *Ils me traitent comme un enfant* | They treat me like a child |
| *Ils me donnent beaucoup de liberté* | They give me lots of freedom |
| *Mon père me critique* | My dad criticises me |
| *J'ai le droit de sortir le soir* | I'm allowed to go out at night |
| *Je n'ai pas le droit de rentrer tard le soir* | I'm not allowed to return home late at night |
| *Je fais ce que je veux* | I do what I like |
| *Ma mère a une bonne influence sur moi* | My mum is a good influence on me |

### Exercise 1

Read the phrases below and decide if they are **vraies** (true) or **fausses** (false) for you and your family relationships.

1. *Je ne m'entends pas bien avec ma famille.*
2. *Je fais ce que je veux chez moi.*
3. *Ma mère me critique tout le temps.*
4. *Mon père me traite comme un enfant.*
5. *J'aime passer du temps avec mes parents.*
6. *Mes parents ne me donnent pas beaucoup de liberté.*
7. *Je n'ai pas le droit de sortir le soir.*

Read the following text about a family of penguins and answer the questions in English.

### Les pingouins en Antarctique

J'habite avec ma mère et mon père en Antarctique, sur un glacier au bord de la mer. Il fait très froid en Antarctique mais nous, les pingouins, sommes habitués au froid ! Des fois, la température est de moins soixante degrés. Les humains pensent que les pingouins sont mignons, mais en réalité nous sommes très forts. Nous habitons la région la plus hostile et froide de la terre ! C'est une vie difficile mais c'est chez nous et je suis heureuse ici.

J'ai passé mon enfance avec mon père. Ma mère était absente parce qu'elle pêchait quand j'étais bébé. Malheureusement, je suis fille unique ! C'est dommage, j'aimerais bien un petit frère !

Mes parents sont mariés depuis six ans et ils sont très fiables et heureux. Ils m'apprennent comment me protéger contre les prédateurs. Mes parents me donnent beaucoup de liberté. Nous avons de petites disputes de temps en temps, comme toutes les familles, mais en général, je m'entends très bien avec mes parents. J'ai vraiment de la chance !

**TOP TIP**

Always read the questions carefully first. Identify the key words and highlight them so that you then know what you're looking for in French.

1. Where do the penguins live? Give details. (3)
2. What does the penguin say about the temperature? (2)
3. What does she say about her parents when she was young? (2)
4. What does she say about brothers and sisters? (2)
5. How does she get on with her parents? Mention any three things. (3)
6. What is the text mainly about? Tick the correct box. (1)

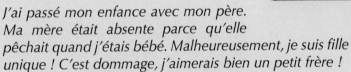

| | |
|---|---|
| 1. How penguins survive in Antarctica | ☐ |
| 2. How penguins support each other | ☐ |
| 3. The family life of penguins | ☐ |

# Friends

You can pick and mix vocabulary about family and friends from pages 14 and 16 to give you a range of ways of describing your relationships.

| | |
|---|---|
| *Mes amis* | My friends |
| *Mon/Ma meilleur(e) ami(e)* | My best friend |
| *J'ai plusieurs meilleur(e)s ami(e)s* | I have several best friends |
| *Mes camarades de classe* | My classmates |
| *Mes ami(e)s proches* | My close friends |
| *On sort ensemble* | We go out together |
| *On parle au téléphone* | We talk on the phone |
| *On s'envoie des SMS* | We text each other |
| *On sort le soir* | We go out in the evening |
| *On discute de tout* | We talk about everything |
| *On a des choses en commun* | We have things in common |
| *On a les mêmes goûts* | We have the same tastes |
| *On rigole ensemble* | We have a laugh |
| *Pour moi, un bon ami c'est quelqu'un ...* | For me a good friend is someone ... |
| *qui a beaucoup d'humour* | with a good sense of humour |
| *qui est fidèle* | who is loyal |
| *qui me comprend* | who understands me |

**TOP TIP**

Focus on learning no more than 10–20 new words or phrases per hour.

## Exercise 1: Les amis

Read the following statements about relationships with family and friends. Think of someone you know who fits this description and write who it is in French in the column provided, for example, Ma mère, mon meilleur ami, etc. If there is no one, you can write 'personne' (nobody). You can refer to the vocabulary on pages 14 and 16 to help you. English translations of the phrases can be found online at https://collins.co.uk/pages/scottish-curriculum-free-resources.

| Phrase | Qui est-ce ? e.g. C'est ma mère |
|---|---|
| 1. *On s'entend bien.* | |
| 2. *On peut parler de tout.* | |
| 3. *Je peux me confier à cette personne.* | |
| 4. *Il/Elle a beaucoup d'humour.* | |
| 5. *Il/Elle me critique tout le temps.* | |
| 6. *On parle souvent au téléphone.* | |
| 7. *On sort le soir.* | |
| 8. *On s'envoie des SMS.* | |
| 9. *On a des choses en commun.* | |
| 10. *On se dispute.* | |

## Exercise 2

Read through the following descriptions of relationships with friends and organise them into two columns under the headings *Un bon ami* and *Un mauvais ami*.

1. *C'est quelqu'un qui a une bonne influence sur moi.*
2. *Je peux me confier à cette personne.*
3. *On se dispute souvent.*
4. *Il me critique beaucoup.*
5. *On ne peut pas parler de tout.*
6. *On ne s'entend pas bien.*
7. *On ne se dispute jamais.*
8. *C'est une personne qui n'a pas une bonne influence sur moi.*
9. *On n'a rien en commun.*
10. *C'est une personne qui est très fidèle.*
11. *Elle ne me comprend pas.*
12. *On rigole ensemble.*

## Exercise 3

Now listen to the conversation between two French teenagers, Sadiq and Adèle, who are talking about their classmates.

What do Sadiq and Adèle think about their friends? Complete the table below.

**Audio tracks to support all listening activities in this book are available to download from the Leckie website. Go to https://collins.co.uk/pages/scottish-curriculum-free-resources-french**

| Friend | Sadiq's opinion | Adèle's opinion |
|---|---|---|
| Christophe<br>Sophie<br>André<br>Max | | |

## Exercise 4

Now read the following text and answer the questions in English.

**Melissa :** *Je trouve que mes amis me comprennent et qu'on peut rigoler ensemble. Nous avons nos blagues à nous et nous nous soutenons les uns les autres, quand par exemple on a des problèmes à l'école ou dans nos vies personnelles. Je passe la plupart du temps avec mes amis à l'école et on essaie toujours de déjeuner ensemble. Ma meilleure amie habite une maison très proche de la mienne, donc généralement nous rentrons ensemble à la fin de la journée scolaire. En dehors de l'école, nous nous retrouvons souvent le soir pour aller voir un film au cinéma ou pour prendre un café quelque part. Sinon, nous faisons nos devoirs chez moi (j'ai une grande chambre rien que pour moi). C'est plus facile quand on travail comme ça !*

1. What does Melissa think of her friends? Mention any three things. (3)
2. Where does she say that they spend most of their time and what do they always try to do together? (2)
3. Where does her best friend live? (1)
4. What do they do outside school? (3)
5. What is the overall theme of this text? Tick the correct box.

> 1. How she spends time with her friends. ☐
> 2. What she talks about with her friends. ☐
> 3. Her friends and family problems. ☐

# Describing family and friends

This section will take you through structures and vocabulary to describe your family and friends.

## Adjectives describing your family and friends

This table of adjectives will help to support you in writing descriptively about your family and friends. It's organised into masculine, feminine, singular and plural to help you learn which spelling of the adjective you should use depending on who you are describing (in this case father, parents, mother, sisters).

| Masculine singular | Masculine plural | Feminine singular | Feminine plural | English |
|---|---|---|---|---|
| *mon père est …* | *mes parents sont …* | *ma mère est …* | *mes soeurs sont …* | My father is/my parents are/my mother is/my sisters are … |
| amusant | amusants | amusante | amusantes | fun |
| autoritaire | autoritaires | autoritaire | autoritaires | bossy |
| bête | bêtes | bête | bêtes | stupid |
| casse-pieds | casse-pieds | casse-pieds | casse-pieds | annoying |
| compréhensif | compréhensifs | compréhensive | compréhensives | understanding |
| drôle | drôles | drôle | drôles | funny |
| égoïste | égoïstes | égoïste | égoïstes | selfish |
| embêtant | embêtants | embêtante | embêtantes | annoying |
| ennuyeux | ennuyeux | ennuyeuse | ennuyeuses | boring |
| gâté | gâtés | gâtée | gâtées | spoilt |
| généreux | généreux | généreuse | généreuses | generous |
| gentil | gentils | gentille | gentilles | kind |
| paresseux | paresseux | paresseuse | paresseuses | lazy |
| sage | sages | sage | sages | sensible |
| sévère | sévères | sévère | sévères | strict |
| sympa | sympas | sympa | sympas | nice |
| têtu | têtus | têtue | têtues | stubborn |
| timide | timides | timide | timides | shy |
| travailleur | travailleurs | travailleuse | travailleuses | hard-working |

## Exercise 1

Use the table opposite to complete any three of the following sentences.

Use at least three adjectives per sentence, e.g. *Ma mère est amusante, généreuse et travailleuse.*

| | |
|---|---|
| *Ma (belle-)mère est …* | My mum (stepmother) is … |
| *Mon (beau-)père est …* | My dad (stepfather) is … . |
| *Mes parents sont …* | My parents are … |
| *Mes parents idéaux seraient …* | My ideal parents would be … |
| *Mon (ma) meilleur(e) ami(e) est …* | My best friend is … |
| *Mes amis sont …* | My friends are … |

## Exercise 2

Make a mind map with at least five different people you know, e.g. *mon père, ma grand-mère, mon professeur d'histoire*, etc. Then come up with as many different phrases as you can to describe each of them.

**TOP TIP**

Use the time phrases (e.g. *quelquefois*) and modifiers (e.g. *très*) to make your sentences more interesting.

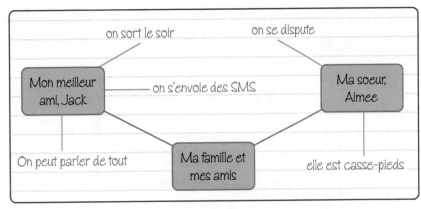

**Grammar blast!**

### être

There are four main irregular verbs in French – *être, avoir, faire, aller*. It's important to know these verbs as they come up frequently.

Let's look at the verb *être* – 'to be', in more detail. It is conjugated in the present tense as below:

| être – to be | | | |
|---|---|---|---|
| *je suis* | I am | *nous sommes* | we are |
| *tu es* | you are | *vous êtes* | you are |
| *il/elle est* | he is | *ils/elles sont* | they are |
| *on est* | one is/we are | | |

### Exercise 3

Read the following text by French rap star, MC Rhéa, talking about family, and see if you can add the missing parts of the verb être.

Je __1__ très connue en France et heureusement j'ai le soutien de ma famille. Nous __2__ une famille très unie et on s'entend bien. Nous sommes quatre dans ma famille : moi, mes parents et ma soeur. Ma soeur, Emma, __3__ plus jeune que moi. Je dirais qu'elle __4__ gentille et travailleuse. Mes parents __5__ mariés depuis vingt ans et habitent une petite île sur la côte atlantique. Mon père __6__ chauffeur routier et il adore écouter tous mes grands hits pendant qu'il __7__ sur la route ! J'ai aussi une nièce, Jessie B. Elle __8__ chanteuse et super cool, comme sa tante ! Finalement, je ne pourrais pas travailler sans mes amis et mon entourage. Nous __9__ une très bonne équipe !

## TOP TIP

Remember, if a sentence begins with one person's name, it takes the il/elle form of a verb. If it starts with two people's names, it takes the ils/elles form.

# Lifestyles 1: healthy and unhealthy eating

The lifestyles topic compares healthy and unhealthy lifestyles. It can make a good talking or writing assessment as it allows you to talk about a variety of things.

## Healthy and unhealthy eating

| | |
|---|---|
| *J'essaie de manger sainement* | I try to eat well |
| *Je mange cinq fruits et légumes par jour* | I eat five fruit and veg a day |
| *Je mange ce que je veux* | I eat what I want |
| *Je mange sainement* | I eat healthily |
| *J'aime manger .../Je n'aime pas manger ...* | I like to eat .../I don't like to eat ... |
| *Je n'aime pas manger* | I don't like to eat |
| *... des bonbons* | ... sweets |
| *... des chips* | ... crisps |
| *... des fruits et légumes* | ... fruit and vegetables |
| *... du poisson* | ... fish |
| *... de la viande* | ... meat |
| *... de la nourriture grasse et sucrée* | ... fatty and sweet foods |
| *... des aliments biologiques* | ... organic food |
| *Je suis végétarien(ne)* | I'm vegetarian |
| *J'ai une alimentation équilibrée* | I have a balanced diet |
| *Je bois huit verres d'eau par jour* | I drink eight glasses of water a day |
| *Je prends le petit-déjeuner le matin* | I eat breakfast in the morning |
| *Je déjeune à la cantine* | I eat lunch at the canteen |

**TOP TIP**

-ER verbs, like manger, which have a 'g' before the 'er', always keep the letter 'e' in the nous form of the verb, e.g. Nous mangeons.

**Exercise 1**

From the sentences below, choose and write out those that reflect your attitude to healthy or unhealthy eating.

1. *J'ai/Je n'ai pas une alimentation équilibrée.*
2. *Je (ne) prends (pas) le (de) petit-déjeuner.*
3. *Je déjeune avec mes amis/à la cantine/au fast-food.*
4. *Je bois ___ verres d'eau par jour/Je ne bois pas d'eau.*
5. *J'aime/Je n'aime pas la nourriture grasse et sucrée.*

Exercise 2

Read the following texts in which French pop stars, Joey Dangereux and Sophie Bienvivre talk about their eating habits. Complete the table below with details of each of their attitudes to food, exercise, smoking, alcohol and any other details you might read.

|  | Joey Dangereux | Sophie Bienvivre |
| --- | --- | --- |
| Food |  |  |
| Alcohol |  |  |
| Smoking |  |  |
| Opinion |  |  |

1. *Alors, mes amis écossais, comment ça va ? C'est moi, Joey Dangereux. Je suis batteur dans un groupe de rock qui s'appelle 'Mauvaise santé'. Nous jouons de la musique rock et nous avons un attitude rock aussi ! Moi, je mange toujours ce que je veux ! Je ne mange jamais de fruits ni de légumes, et comme nous sommes souvent en tournée (pour les concerts), je mange beaucoup de malbouffe comme des hamburgers, des pizzas et des frites; recouvertes de mayonnaise bien sûr ! Comme nous sommes un groupe de rock, nous buvons beaucoup d'alcool et nous fumons tous au moins vingt cigarettes par jour. Je suis une rock star, donc la santé n'est pas du tout importante pour moi.*

2. *Bonjour, je m'appelle Sophie Bienvivre et je suis chanteuse. C'est important pour moi de soigner mon apparence et j'essaie d'être toujours en forme. Pour garder la forme, je suis un régime assez strict. Je mange beaucoup de fruits et de légumes (j'adore la salade) et j'évite de manger de la nourriture grasse ou trop salée. J'aime les sucreries et de temps en temps je mange un bonbon ou un gâteau, mais ça n'arrive pas souvent. Je bois très rarement de l'alcool ; seulement un verre de champagne de temps en temps, avec ma famille à Noël par exemple. Quant à la cigarette, je ne fume jamais et je ne supporte pas cela. Je dirais que je suis en très bonne santé mais des fois, je pense que c'est un peu ennuyeux de vivre comme ça. La vie, c'est mieux avec une part de gâteau de temps en temps.*

# Lifestyles 2: sport and exercise

The following vocabulary covers some popular sports. Remember to check if it takes faire or jouer.

| Je fais, je joue ou je pratique ? | Sport (French) | Sport (English) |
|---|---|---|
| Je joue | au foot | football |
| | au hockey | hockey |
| | au basket | basketball |
| | au golf | golf |
| | au ping-pong | table tennis |
| Je fais | de la natation | swimming |
| | de la randonnée | hill-walking |
| | de la voile | sailing |
| | de l'équitation | horse-riding |
| | du vélo | cycling |
| | du VTT | mountain biking |
| | des promenades | walking |
| Je pratiquer | des sports d'hiver | winter sports |
| | des sports nautiques | water sports |

**TOP TIP**

jouer is a regular – ER verb meaning 'to play' and, generally, it goes with sports that are ball sports. Always double-check though, as there are some exceptions!

## Exercise 1

Listen to the following report from the French secondary school lycée Trèsactif in the town of Gardez-la-forme. The school has recently surveyed 100 local residents to see which sports are most popular in the town. Note down the sports mentioned and the numbers of people who do them.

| Sport | Number of people |
|---|---|
| 1. | |
| 2. | |
| 3. | |
| 4. | |
| 5. | |
| 6. | |
| 7. | |
| 8. | |

## Exercise 2

Now read the following opinions about sport. Match the statements to the correct person below by ticking the box.

**Sandrine :** *Je ne suis pas une personne naturellement sportive, mais je reconnais qu'il est important d'être actif et de faire bouger son corps régulièrement.*

**Daniel :** *Pour moi, le sport, c'est essentiel. Si je ne fais pas assez de sport, je deviens un peu grincheux et agité.*

**Caroline :** *J'aime faire du sport mais je n'aime pas le regarder à la télé. Je trouve ça vraiment ennuyeux.*

**Hector :** *Moi j'aime surtout les sports qu'on pratique en plein air. Ça fait du bien d'être au soleil et de respirer l'air frais !*

| | Sandrine | Daniel | Caroline | Hector |
|---|---|---|---|---|
| 1. If I don't do enough sport, I become grumpy and restless. | | | | |
| 2. I don't like to watch it. | | | | |
| 3. I'm not a naturally sporty person. | | | | |
| 4. I especially like sports you do outdoors. | | | | |
| 5. It's important to be active and move your body regularly. | | | | |

**Grammar blast!**

### faire

Faire is one of the most commonly used irregular verbs in French. It means both 'to do' and 'to make' in English.

| faire (to do/to make) | | | |
|---|---|---|---|
| *je fais* | I do/make | *nous faisons* | we do/make |
| *tu fais* | you do/make | *vous faites* | you do/make |
| *il/elle fait* | he/she does/makes | *ils/elles font* | they do/make |
| *on fait* | one does/makes<br>we do/make | | |

## Exercise 3

Using the verb faire and the sports vocabulary, translate the following sentences into French. Remember, where in English we would say 'I go sailing', the French would say 'I do sailing'!

1. We go sailing.
2. You (informal) go horse-riding.
3. They (girls) go mountain-biking.
4. They (boys) go hill-walking.
5. She goes swimming.

| | |
|---|---|
| *Je fais du sport __ fois par semaine* | I exercise __ times a week |
| *Pour rester en forme ...* | To keep in shape ... |
| *Je fais partie d'une équipe de (foot)* | I'm in a (football) club |
| *Je vais à la gym/au centre sportif* | I go to the gym/sport centre |
| *Je suis en forme* | I'm in good shape |
| *Je dois faire plus de sport* | I should do more sport |
| *Je déteste faire du sport* | I hate doing sport |
| *Je soigne mon apparence* | I take care of my appearance |
| *Ça me maintient en forme* | It keeps me in shape |

## Exercise 4

Using the sports vocabulary in this section, write a short paragraph to describe your own attitude to sport. Check the reading and listening exercises for extra phrases you could use. The example below will help you.

*Je suis une personne naturellement sportive. Pour rester en forme, je fais beaucoup de sport. Je fais du footing le week-end avec mon petit frère. J'aime le footing parce que ça me maintient en forme. Je fais aussi de la natation deux fois par semaine.*

### *TOP TIP*

Using time phrases gives your writing structure and makes it more interesting, e.g. *Nous faisons du ski de temps en temps*.

# Lifestyles 3: unhealthy lifestyles

The final section in the lifestyles topic looks at unhealthy lifestyles.

*C'est bon pour la santé* — It's good for your health
*C'est mauvais pour la santé* — It's bad for your health
*Je ne supporte pas les cigarettes* — I can't stand cigarettes
*Je fume __ cigarettes par jour* — I smoke __ cigarettes a day
*Je trouve que fumer c'est ...* — I think smoking is ...
  *... horrible* — ... horrible
  *... dégoûtant* — ... disgusting
*Cela nuit à la santé* — It's harmful for your health
*Pour être en bonne santé il ne faut pas ...* — To be in good health you must not ...
  *... fumer des cigarettes* — ... smoke cigarettes
  *... boire trop de boissons sucrées* — ... drink too many sugary drinks
  *... boire trop d'alcool* — ... drink too much alcohol
  *... prendre de la drogue* — ... take drugs
  *... manger trop de gâteaux et de bonbons* — ... eat too many cakes and sweets
  *... manger beaucoup de nourriture grasse* — ... eat a lot of fatty food
  *... manger trop de nourriture salée* — ... eat too much salty food

**Grammar blast!**

## Negatives

Saying 'you must' or 'you must not' is easy in French. It's simply a case of using either 'il faut' or 'il ne faut pas' and then following it with the full infinitive form of the verb. For example, 'il faut manger' – 'you must eat' – and 'il ne faut pas manger' – 'you must not eat'.

### Exercise 1

Using the vocabulary above to help you, write the following phrases in French.

1. You must not take drugs.
2. You must not smoke cigarettes.
3. You must be in good health.
4. You must not eat a lot of cakes and sweets.
5. You must not drink too much alcohol.

*TOP TIP*

Make verb cards with the French on one side of a piece of card and the English on the other. Keep these as a set and use them to revise the words.

## Exercise 2

Read the following article about health by Bernard Le But, a famous French footballer, in the French magazine *La Forme*, and then answer the questions about Bernard's attitude to health and well-being in English.

1. Why does Bernard think it's important to be in good shape?
2. What five pieces of advice does Bernard give you with regard to health? Give details.

**TOP TIP**

Always include all details in order to get a mark! E.g. don't miss out time phrases like 'tous les jours' or modifiers such as très, assez, etc.

*Pour moi, il est essentiel de se maintenir en forme. Non seulement parce que je suis joueur de foot, mais aussi parce que j'aime me sentir bien et parce que je trouve que c'est bon pour la santé mentale en général.*

*Si j'avais des conseils à vous donner, je pense que je dirais qu'il faut manger sainement (beaucoup de fruits et légumes tous les jours et pas trop de bonbons, bien sûr), ne pas boire trop d'alcool (en France on boit du vin mais c'est avec modération je dirais), trouver des sports que vous aimez et les pratiquer régulièrement (la natation ou le vélo par exemple), marcher au lieu de prendre la voiture ou le bus et surtout, éviter de fumer. Les Français ont la réputation de fumer beaucoup et je déteste ça.*

## Exercise 3

Now look at the text again and see if you can find the French for the following phrases:

1. It is essential to stay in good shape.
2. It's good for your mental health.
3. If I had advice to give you.
4. Do regularly
5. Avoid smoking
6. French people have a reputation for smoking a lot.

# Media

The media topic looks at what media you use in your daily life.

## Les médias

| | |
|---|---|
| *Je regarde la télé* | I watch TV |
| *Je regarde des films* | I watch films |
| *Je surfe sur Internet* | I surf the Internet |
| *J'écoute la radio* | I listen to the radio |
| *J'écoute de la musique* | I listen to music |
| *Je lis des journaux/le journal* | I read the papers |
| *Je lis des livres* | I read books |
| *Je lis des magazines* | I read magazines |
| *Je vais au cinéma* | I go to the cinema |

## Exercise 1

Using the time phrases below, write sentences showing how often you do different activities. Looking at our examples, pay attention to where the time phrases go.

**TOP TIP**

When using 'ne ... jamais' sandwich the verb between 'ne' and 'jamais' to make it negative, e.g. 'je ne vais jamais', 'je ne lis jamais' and 'je ne surfe jamais'.

| Time phrase | English | Our example |
|---|---|---|
| *Tous les jours* | Everyday | *Je lis le journal **tous les jours**.* |
| *Une ou deux fois par semaine* | Once or twice a week | *Je vais au cinéma **une ou deux fois par semaine**.* |
| *Souvent* | Often | *Je lis **souvent** des livres.* |
| *Le soir* | In the evening | *J'écoute la radio **le soir**.* |
| *Après l'école* | After school | *Je regarde des films **après l'école**.* |
| *Ne ... jamais* | Never | *Je **ne** regarde **jamais** la télévision.* |

 ### *L'Internet*

| | |
|---|---|
| *Internet* | The Internet |
| *un site web* | a website |
| *Mes sites web préférés sont ...* | My favourite websites are ... |
| *en ligne* | online |
| *un internaute* | an internet user |
| *des réseaux sociaux* | social networks |
| *Je suis sur Facebook* | I'm on Facebook |
| *Je suis discret (discrète)* | I'm a private person |
| *Je suis ____ sur Twitter* | I follow ____ on Twitter |
| *Je chatte avec des amis en ligne* | I chat with friends online |
| *J'écris un blog* | I write a blog |

**TOP TIP**

When you are talking about the Internet, as in the World Wide Web, it is a proper noun and so takes a capital I in both French and English.

**TOP TIP**

'Je suis' can mean both 'I am' and 'I follow'.

### Exercise 2

How do you feel about the Internet? Read this online forum exchange to find out more about how some French people feel about using the Internet.

 ***FrançoisCocoNuméroUno :*** *Moi, j'aime beaucoup surfer sur Internet. Je passe des heures sur des sites web à lire et chercher des informations. Je pense que j'y passe environ quatre ou cinq heures par jour. Je surfe et je regarde la télé en même temps.*

***Tout_est_très_simple :*** *J'essaie de limiter le temps que je passe sur Internet chaque jour. A mon avis, c'est très facile de devenir un peu accro à Internet et j'essaie d'éviter de passer des heures et des heures sur des sites comme Facebook. J'ai l'application Facebook sur mon téléphone portable et sur ma tablette, donc je suis tout le temps tenté de consulter ce site.*

***Monsieur.Point.Com :*** *J'adore Internet. Je suis sur Internet toute la journée. Je cherche des informations sur Internet pour mes études, je fais du shopping sur Internet, je chatte avec mes amis, je regarde la télé et des films sur Internet, je joue à des jeux vidéo en ligne et j'écoute de la musique sur Internet.*

***Chat_vs_Chien :*** *Je préfère faire autre chose plutôt que d'aller sur Internet et je n'ai pas envie d'être devant un écran d'ordinateur toute la journée. Je n'ai pas de compte Facebook ou Twitter parce que je suis une personne discrète et que je n'ai pas envie de partager tous les détails de ma vie. Je préfère que ma vie privée reste privée.*

Copy out the table below and organise at least 20 phrases from the texts into the table to show which reflect your use of the Internet: *'C'est comme moi'* (It's like me) or *'Ce n'est pas comme moi'* (It's not like me).

| *C'est comme moi* | *Ce n'est pas comme moi* |
|---|---|
| | |

# New technologies

Now let's look at other forms of technology that we use regularly.

**TOP TIP**

Writing a bit of French every day and building up a bank of key phrases you can use in assessments is an effective way to revise for writing.

| | |
|---|---|
| J'ai (un téléphone portable). | I have (a mobile phone). |
| ... une tablette. | ... a tablet. |
| ... un ordinateur. | ... a computer. |
| ... un ordinateur portable. | ... a laptop. |
| ... une liseuse. | ... an E-reader. |
| J'envoie des SMS. | I send texts. |
| Je télécharge des applis. | I download apps. |
| Les (téléphones) portables sont très utiles. | Mobile phones are very useful. |
| Les nouvelles technologies améliorent nos vies. | New technology improves our lives. |
| On peut faire du shopping de chez soi. | We can shop from home. |
| On peut trouver des informations en ligne sur tout. | We can find information about everything online. |
| On peut communiquer avec des amis/de la famille à l'étranger. | We can communicate with friends/family abroad. |
| On peut organiser ses vacances en ligne. | We can organise holidays online. |
| Il faut beaucoup d'énergie pour fabriquer toute cette technologie. | A lot of energy is needed to make all this technology. |
| Ça coûte cher. | It's expensive. |
| La cyberintimidation est un gros problème. | Cyberbullying is a big problem. |

## Exercise 1

What technology do you use in your daily life? Look at the lists below and tick the things you do and how often you do them.

| Nouvelle technologie | Plusieurs fois par jour | Plusieurs fois par semaine | Ne ... jamais |
|---|---|---|---|
| J'utilise mon téléphone portable. | | | |
| J'envoie des SMS. | | | |
| Je lis des livres avec une liseuse. | | | |
| Je télécharge des applis. | | | |
| Je surfe sur Internet avec un ordinateur portable. | | | |
| Je surfe sur Internet avec un téléphone portable. | | | |
| Je fais du shopping en ligne. | | | |

Now use the table above to write five sentences describing how you use technology in your daily life. Include a time phrase in each one.

Don't forget when using 'ne ... jamais' that you have to sandwich this around the verb! For example, 'Je ne fais jamais de shopping en ligne.'

## Exercise 2

Listen to Guilluame and his wife, Christine, talking about technology and then answer the questions in English.

1. Guillaume suggests three presents for Christine's 60th birthday. What does he suggest? Mention any two things. (2)
2. a) What type of computer does Christine mention? (1)
   b) What is wrong with her current mobile phone? Mention any one thing. (1)
3. What does Guillaume think of new technology? (2)
4. What does Christine like about new technology? Mention any three things. (3)
5. What does Guillaume decide to buy for Christine? (1)
6. What does she ask him to get? (1)
7. What condition does Guillaume put on the present? (1)

Now check your answers. Make sure you've included all details.

# Global languages

The global languages topic looks at the importance of language learning. As you are developing your skills as a linguist, it's important that you have an awareness of the advantages these skills bring and how these can benefit you in your career and wider prospects.

## My languages

| Mes langues | My languages |
|---|---|
| Je parle __ langues | I speak __ languages |
| Je suis bilingue | I'm bilingual |
| Je suis multilingue | I'm multilingual |
| Ma langue maternelle c'est le ... | My mother tongue is ... |
| J'apprends (l'espagnol) | I'm learning (Spanish) |
| Je parle français depuis six ans | I've been speaking French for 6 years |
| Je parle aussi l'allemand | I also speak German |
| Je parle un peu le ... | I speak a bit of ... |
| Ma langue préférée c'est le français | My favourite language is French |
| Je voudrais apprendre le russe | I would like to learn Russian |
| Le chinois est plus difficile que le français | Mandarin is more difficult than French |

### Exercise 1

What are your experiences of language learning? Complete the language portfolio below with your skills and experience and tick the level you consider yourself to be for each language.

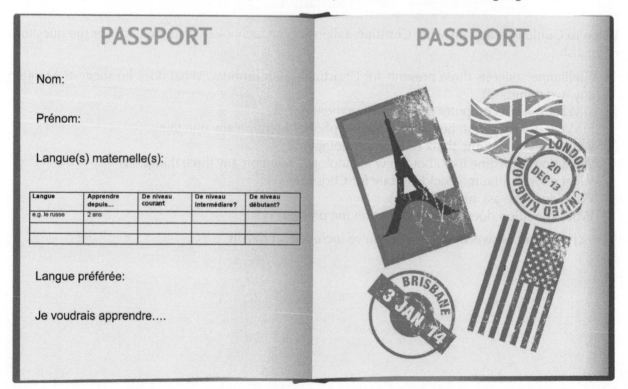

PASSPORT

PASSPORT

Nom:

Prénom:

Langue(s) maternelle(s):

| Langue | Apprendre depuis... | De niveau courant | De niveau intermédiare? | De niveau débutant? |
|---|---|---|---|---|
| e.g. le russe | 2 ans | | | |
| | | | | |
| | | | | |

Langue préférée:

Je voudrais apprendre....

## Exercise 2

Listen to young people from countries around the world speaking about their experiences of language learning. Copy and complete the table below with the missing information for each of the texts. Give as many details as you can.

Hint: Berber is a language native to North Africa.

| Name | Where they live | Languages spoken | Opinion of languages |
|------|-----------------|------------------|----------------------|
| **Annas** | | | |
| **Ryuichi** | | | |
| **Steffie** | | | |

> **TOP TIP**
>
> Read through the vocabulary lists before you do any listening and try saying the phrases out loud. This will help tune your brain to the language and revise the sounds before you listen.

## Exercise 3

Now read the text below about a Scottish zoologist's experience of language learning and then come up with your own set of 10 questions about the text. Think about how many marks you will allocate to each question and what kind of details you would expect in the answers. The first one is done for you below.

*Je m'appelle Donald et je viens d'un petit village dans les îles Hébrides. Je parlais l'anglais à la maison mais à l'école primaire, tous les cours étaient en gaélique. J'ai donc grandi en étant bilingue sans vraiment m'en rendre compte. Au collège, j'ai appris le français et l'allemand, mais je ne pensais pas que j'étais très fort en langues. J'avais du mal à me souvenir de tous les mots et j'étais parfois nerveux quand il fallait parler devant les autres ; c'est normal, je crois. Après avoir fini le lycée, je suis allé à la fac pour étudier les animaux, ma grande passion dans la vie ! Bien sûr, je ne pensais pas du tout que les langues m'aideraient. Mais, me voilà, dix ans plus tard en train de travailler dans une équipe de scientifiques qui vient du monde entier. Aujourd'hui, par exemple, je travaille sur un bateau en plein milieu de la mer du Nord (on fait des recherches sur les phoques). On est 50 personnes au total sur ce bateau, et au moins huit nationalités différentes, y compris des Philippins, des Russes, des Français, deux Canadiens, un Allemand, une Japonaise et moi, l'Ecossais ! Ici, on travaille principalement en anglais mais j'essaie d'apprendre et de parler un peu toutes les langues. Par conséquent, je trouve que je m'entends mieux avec mes camarades. C'est un petit geste, mais ça montre que je m'intéresse aux autres et à leur culture. Ce bateau nous montre que nous habitons une petite planète de nos jours. Le monde est très petit !*

| Question | Marks | Answer |
|----------|-------|--------|
| 1.  Where is Donald from? | 2 | A **small** village in the Hebrides. |
|  |  |  |

# The importance of language learning

What's so important about language learning? This section will start to look at this in a bit more depth and explore some of the reasons why languages matter to us all.

| | |
|---|---|
| *Les langues sont importantes (parce que) ...* <br>     *... les employeurs et les entreprises cherchent des employés qui ont des aptitudes linguistiques* <br>     *... pour l'économie de l'Ecosse* <br>     *... il y a des avantages cognitifs* | Languages are important (because) ... <br>     ... employers and businesses are looking for employees with language skills <br>     ... for Scotland's economy <br>     ... there are cognitive benefits |
| *Quand on parle plusieurs langues, on donne l'impression d'être ...* <br>     *... intelligent* <br>     *... un communicant efficace* <br>     *... ouvert aux autres et aux autres cultures* <br>     *... intéressé par le monde* | When we speak several languages we give the impression of being ... <br>     ... intelligent <br>     ... an effective communicator <br>     ... open to other people and cultures <br>     ... interested in the world |
| *Les langues nous permettent de ...* <br>     *... communiquer avec des gens venus de différents pays* <br>     *... comprendre différentes cultures* <br>     *... travailler à l'étranger* <br>     *... gagner plus d'argent* <br>     *... être compétitif sur le marché du travail mondial* | Languages enable us to ... <br>     ... communicate with people from different countries <br>     ... understand different cultures <br>     ... work abroad <br>     ... earn more money <br>     ... compete in a global job market |
| *Apprendre une langue, c'est amusant* | Learning a language is fun |
| *Tout le monde doit apprendre une deuxième langue* | Everyone should learn a second language |

## Exercise 1

Make a set of individual vocabulary cards with the French on one side and the English on the other. Lay them out on a table and test yourself by reading the French, saying what it is and then flipping the cards over to see if you're correct. Once you know the French, see if you can do it in reverse with the English face up.

**TOP TIP**

Do this exercise activity for every topic. Collect a set for each topic and then jumble them up all the topics at the end to see if you can still remember them when they're mixed up.

## Exercise 2

Read the following statistics about languages. Choose the missing words and phrases from the box below to complete the sentences.

| | | | |
|---|---|---|---|
| *les plus utiles* | *une barrière* | *des pays qui ne parlent* | *les compétences* |
| *a comprendre les* | *gagnent plus que* | *pas l'anglais* | *linguistiques* |
| *différences culturelles* | *ne parle pas du tout* | *besoin de* | *seulement* |
| *la population mondiale* | *anglais* | *d'Internet* | *L'économie britannique* |
| *connaissances culturelles* | *un pays multilingue* | *les marchés étrangers* | *une langue étrangère* |

1. *Une entreprise sur quatre préfère un employé qui parle _____.*
2. *En moyenne, après 3 ans de travail, les diplômés en langues _____ les diplômés en maths, ingénierie, physique, chimie et astronomie.*
3. *Le français, l'allemand et l'espagnol sont les langues considérées comme _____ par les patrons.*
4. *L'Ecosse est _____. On parle plus de 160 langues en Ecosse.*
5. *76% des patrons ne sont pas satisfaits par _____des candidats à l'emploi.*
6. *61% des patrons pensent que les candidats à l'emploi n'ont pas assez de _____.*
7. *Les trois quarts des entreprises ont _____ candidats à l'emploi qui ont des compétences linguistiques.*
8. *80% des entreprises ne sont pas capables de faire des affaires avec _____ parce qu'elles ne parlent pas les langues étrangères.*
9. *Deux entreprises sur trois disent que les langues sont _____.*
10. *Huit sur dix disent qu'elles ont des difficultés _____.*
11. *72% du commerce britannique international concerne _____.*
12. *_____ pourrait gagner £21 milliards de plus par an si on améliorait nos compétences linguistiques.*
13. *6% de _____ parle anglais.*
14. *75% de la population mondiale _____.*
15. *En Grande-Bretagne, _____ une personne sur dix parle une langue étrangère.*
16. *Seulement 29% _____ est en anglais.*

**TOP TIP**

'Un sur dix' means 'one out of ten'. Make sure you know your numbers for statistics, percentages and times. These are common features of assessments.

# Citizenship 1: my home town

## My town

Let's start by looking at vocabulary you can use to describe your home town.

| | |
|---|---|
| Ma ville | My town |
| c'est situé | it's situated |
| se trouve | is found |
| au bord de la mer | by the coast |
| au bord d'un lac | by a lake |
| à la montagne | in the mountains |
| à la campagne | in the countryside |
| c'est une grande ville | it's a large town/city |
| c'est loin de | it's far from |
| c'est pittoresque | it's picturesque |
| historique | historic |
| touristique | touristic |
| industriel(le) | industrial |
| animé(e) | lively |
| culturel(le) | cultural |

### Exercise 1

Make a list of five towns and cities you know or have visited either in Scotland or abroad. Brainstorm at least 10 adjectives and phrases to describe them (more if you can though) and then use these to write a short paragraph to describe each of them. Try and expand on the vocabulary given above to stretch yourself.

### Exercise 2

Look at the following places in a town.

| | | |
|---|---|---|
| un château | des magasins | une patinoire |
| un lac | une cathédrale | un stade |
| des monuments historiques | une église | un centre sportif |
| un théâtre | un musée | une plage |
| un jardin | un cinéma | un parc |
| des cafés | une rivière | |
| des restaurants | un office du tourisme | |

Thinking about your own town, and using a dictionary to help you, sort them into the two headings, 'il y a' and 'il n'y a pas de' as has been done in the table below.

Don't forget that after 'il n'y a pas de', we don't add 'un' or 'une', e.g. 'il n'y a pas de château'.

| Il y a | Il n'y a pas de |
|---|---|
| E.g. Il y a des restaurants | E.g. Il n'y a pas de plage |

**TOP TIP**

Draw a rough map of your town and label the different areas in French. This will help you to associate the vocabulary with something you are familiar with.

**TOP TIP**

Looking up French tourist sites can help you write more interesting French about your town. Do a search online for your town followed by 'visiter + tourisme' and you may well find French tourist sites you can read through and borrow phrases from.

## Town and country living

This vocabulary compares life in the country with life in a town. Which do you prefer? Note that all the adjectives are feminine here as they relate to **la** campagne and **la** ville.

| | |
|---|---|
| *Je préfère habiter en ville* | I prefer living in the town |
| *Je préfère habiter à la campagne* | I prefer living in the country |
| *La ville est plus ___ que la campagne* | The town is more __ than the country |
| *animée* | lively |
| *intéressante* | interesting |
| *polluée* | polluted |
| *dangereuse* | dangerous |
| *Il y a beaucoup de choses à faire* | There is lots to do |
| *La campagne est plus __ que la ville* | The country is more __ than the town |
| *jolie* | pretty |
| *pittoresque* | picturesque |
| *calme* | calm |
| *tranquille* | quiet |

**Grammar blast!**

### Comparatives – plus que and moins que

You can easily say something is 'more or less than' in French by using 'plus que' and 'moins que'. These are called comparatives. Here are a couple of examples:

- *Ma mère est **moins** compréhensive **que** mon père.*
- *La ville est **plus** animée **que** la campagne.*
- *Le château est **plus** petit **que** la tour.*

Don't forget that the adjective you're using in the middle of the sentence has to agree with whatever comes first, e.g. ***La voiture** est moins **lente** que la velo.* 'La voiture' is feminine so the word for slow is spelled in the feminine form, lent**e**.

### Exercise 3

Complete these sentences with 'plus que' or 'moins que'.

1. *La ville est _____ polluée ___ la campagne.*
2. *La campagne est _____ calme _____ la ville.*
3. *La ville est ___ peuplée ___ la campagne.*

And now complete the following sentences with the correct adjective agreement.

4. *La campagne est plus (joli) que la ville.*
5. *La ville est moins (bruyant) que la campagne.*
6. *La campagne est plus (tranquille) que la ville.*

# Citizenship 2: the environment

Environmental issues are global issues and affect us all. They are as much of a hot topic in France as in Scotland, so let's now look at some of the vocabulary we would use when talking about them.

| | |
|---|---|
| *il ne faut pas .../il faut ...* | you must not .../you must ... |
| ... *économiser l'énergie* | ... save energy |
| ... *gaspiller l'eau* | ... waste water |
| ... *recycler les déchets* | ... recycle waste |
| ... *économiser le papier* | ... save paper |
| ... *éteindre les lumières* | ... switch off the lights |
| ... *acheter des produits bios* | ... buy organic products |
| ... *acheter des produits écologiques* | ... buy green products |
| ... *jeter les papiers par terre* | ... drop litter |
| ... *prendre les transports en commun* | ... use public transport |
| ... *marcher au lieu de prendre la voiture* | ... walk instead of taking the car |
| ... *protéger la planète* | ... protect the planet |
| *je recycle* | I recycle |
| ... *le papier* | ... paper |
| ... *les plastiques* | ... plastic |
| ... *le verre* | ... glass |
| ... *les emballages* | ... packaging |
| ... *les restes de nourriture* | ... food waste |
| ... *les appareils électroniques* | ... electronics |
| ... *les piles* | ... batteries |
| ... *les vêtements* | ... clothes |
| ... *les chaussures* | ... shoes |

## Exercise 1

Decide whether you would use either 'il faut' or 'il ne faut pas' for each of the following pieces of eco-advice and rewrite them in full. For example, 'Il faut marcher au lieu de prendre la voiture'.

1. *économiser l'énergie*
2. *gaspiller l'eau*
3. *recycler les déchets*
4. *économiser le papier*
5. *éteindre les lumières*

## Grammar blast!

### Negatives

The following negatives are common features in reading and listening at National 5.

| Negative | Meaning | Example |
|---|---|---|
| *Ne ... pas* | not/don't/does not/doesn't | *Je ne fais pas* – I don't do |
| *Ne ... jamais* | never | *Je ne fais jamais* – I never do |
| *Ne ... plus* | any longer/no more | *Je ne le fais plus* – I don't do any longer |
| *Ne ... que* | only | *Je ne fais que* – I only do |
| *Ne ... rien* | nothing | *Je ne fais rien* – I do nothing |
| *Ne ... aucun* | any | *Je n'ai aucune idée* – I don't have any idea |

To form these negatives, the verb is sandwiched between 'ne' and the ending (e.g. rien).

Je ne    joue    plus

**TOP TIP**

Think of this as a negative sandwich; **ne** and the ending are the bread and the verb is the filling in the middle!

Look at the examples below showing how verbs become negative.

| | |
|---|---|
| *Je joue* (I play) | *Je ne joue plus* (I don't play any longer) |
| *Je regarde* (I watch) | *Je ne regarde jamais* (I never watch) |
| *J'entends* (I hear) | *Je n'entends rien* (I hear nothing) |
| *J'ai* (I have) | *Je n'ai que* (I only have) |

When **je** is followed by a vowel, it becomes **j'**, e.g. **J'**écoute. Similarly, when **ne** is followed by a vowel it becomes **n'**. So if you want to make a verb that begins with a vowel negative (e.g. écouter) it would become 'je **n'**écoute' (plus an ending such as **pas**) as the **ne** part now comes directly before the vowel.

### Exercise 2

Change these phrases using the negatives in brackets.

1. *J'éteins les lumières* (don't)
2. *Il gaspille de l'énergie* (only)
3. *Nous prenons les transports en commun* (never)
4. *J'achète des produits bios* (no longer)
5. *Elle recycle* (nothing)

**TOP TIP**

Using a range of negatives in your writing will also show a degree of sophistication, which will help you pick up extra marks.

Exercise 3

Listen to the conversation between two residents of the rue du monde, Mme Vert and M. le Gaspillage. Answer the questions below in English.

1. What does Mme Vert say are now in their street? (1)
2. What does M. Le Gaspillage recycle? (1)
3. What is his attitude to saving energy? Mention any one thing. (1)
4. What kind of products does Mme Vert only buy? (1)
5. What type of products does M. Le Gaspillage buy? Mention any 2 things. (2)
6. What does he say about using the car? (1)

# Focus on grammar: present tense – regular and irregular verbs

This section will look at the present tense in a bit more depth. What is it? The **present tense** is used to describe things that are happening **now.**

## Regular verbs in the present tense

Let's start by looking at how this is formed with regular verbs.

The majority of French verbs are regular, and the good news is that these are the verbs that like to follow the rules! Once you've learned these rules, you can then apply them to most French verbs.

> **The three main groups of regular verbs are:**
> * **ER verbs**
> * **RE verbs**
> * **IR verbs**

To conjugate these verbs, you simply remove the two last letters (-er, -re or -ir) from the infinitive and then add the following endings:

|            | ER Verbs  | RE Verbs  | IR Verbs  |
|------------|-----------|-----------|-----------|
|            | *parler*  | *attendre*| *finir*   |
| *je/j'*    | *parle*   | *attends* | *finis*   |
| *tu*       | *parles*  | *attends* | *finis*   |
| *il/elle/on* | *parle* | *attend*  | *finit*   |
| *nous*     | *parlons* | *attendons* | *finissons* |
| *vous*     | *parlez*  | *attendez* | *finissez* |
| *ils/elles* | *parlent* | *attendent* | *finissent* |

**TOP TIP**

Don't forget that the 'ent' ending of the 'ils' and 'elles' forms is always silent in spoken French.

## Exercise 1

Reorganise the following common regular ER, RE and IR verbs under the correct headings and add the English translation for each of them.

| ER | RE | IR |
|---|---|---|
| réussir | bavarder | maigrir |
| travailler | grossir | regarder |
| trouver | chercher | rentrer |
| vendre | acheter | oublier |
| réfléchir | perdre | entendre |
| donner | habiter | aimer |

**TOP TIP**

Watch out for verbs with accents, like préférer. In the present tense the second acute accent becomes a grave accent, e.g. Je préfère.

## Exercise 2

Now choose the correct verb from the table above and then conjugate it to complete the following sentences.

1. Je _____ quand je mange beaucoup de nourriture grasse et sucrée.
2. Il _____ tout le temps avec sa meilleure amie !
3. Ils _____ des films pendant leur temps libre.
4. Ma mère n' _____ que des produits bios au supermarché.
5. Ma famille et moi _____ dans une grande ville animée et historique dans le sud de la France.

# Irregular verbs in the present tense

The irregular verbs are the ones which are a bit more awkward and do their own thing – they don't follow rules but there are recognisable patterns. It's just a case of learning them. The four most common irregular verbs are below.

| être – to be | | | |
|---|---|---|---|
| je suis | I am | nous sommes | we are |
| tu es | you are | vous êtes | you are |
| il/elle est | he/she is | ils/elles sont | they are |
| on est | one is/we are | | |

| faire – to do/to make | | | |
|---|---|---|---|
| je fais | I do/make | nous faisons | we do/make |
| tu fais | you do/make | vous faites | you do/make |
| il/elle fait | he/she does/makes | ils/elles font | they do/make |
| on fait | one does/makes we do/make | | |

| aller – to go | | | |
|---|---|---|---|
| je vais | I go | nous allons | we go |
| tu vas | you go | vous allez | you go |
| il/elle va | he/she goes | ils/elles vont | they go |
| on va | one goes/we go | | |

| avoir – to have | | | |
|---|---|---|---|
| j'ai | I have | nous avons | we have |
| tu as | you have | vous avez | you have |
| il/elle a | he/she has | ils/elles ont | they have |
| on a | one has/we have | | |

## Exercise 3

Read the following text and complete the sentences with the missing pronouns and verbs conjugated in the present tense.

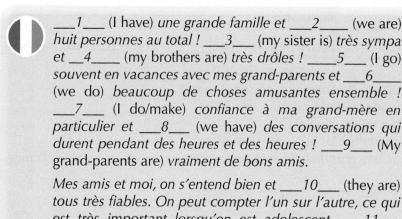

___1___ (I have) *une grande famille et* ___2___ (we are) *huit personnes au total !* ___3___ (my sister is) *très sympa et* ___4___ (my brothers are) *très drôles !* ___5___ (I go) *souvent en vacances avec mes grand-parents et* ___6___ (we do) *beaucoup de choses amusantes ensemble !* ___7___ (I do/make) *confiance à ma grand-mère en particulier et* ___8___ (we have) *des conversations qui durent pendant des heures et des heures !* ___9___ (My grand-parents are) *vraiment de bons amis.*

*Mes amis et moi, on s'entend bien et* ___10___ (they are) *tous très fiables. On peut compter l'un sur l'autre, ce qui est très important lorsqu'on est adolescent.* ___11___ (I have) *de la chance d'avoir une famille et des amis qui* ___12___ (are) *aussi sympas.*

**TOP TIP**

Say verbs over repeatedly, add a rhythm or a tune, write them out repeatedly or make cards to play matching pairs games to revise them. Songs on video-hosting sites such as YouTube can be useful for learning verbs.

## Modal verbs

Modal verbs are verbs that express a mood such as want, need or possibility. The main modal verbs we are going to focus on are:

- *devoir* (to have to)
- *pouvoir* (to be able to)
- *vouloir* (to want to)

There are similarities in how these verbs are formed. Again, you just have to learn this for each of them. The conjugations are in the table below for you to refer to.

| devoir – to have to | | | |
|---|---|---|---|
| je dois | I have to | nous devons | we have to |
| tu dois | you have to | vous devez | you have to |
| il/elle doit | he/she has to | ils/elles doivent | they have to |
| on doit | one has to<br>we have to | | |

| pouvoir – to be able to | | | |
|---|---|---|---|
| *je peux* | I can | *nous pouvons* | we can |
| *tu peux* | you can | *vous pouvez* | you can |
| *il/elle peut* | he/she can | *ils/elles peuvent* | they can |
| *on peut* | one can/we can | | |

| vouloir – to want to | | | |
|---|---|---|---|
| *je veux* | I want to | *nous voulons* | we want to |
| *tu veux* | you want to | *vous voulez* | you want to |
| *il/elle veut* | he/she wants to | *ils/elles veulent* | they want to |
| *on veut* | one wants to/we want to | | |

## Exercise 4

Create three sets of cards.

- Set one: pronouns, e.g. *je, tu, il, elle, on, nous, vous, ils* and *elles*.
- Set two: verb conjugations, e.g. *dois, dois, doit, doit, doit, devons, devez, doivent.*
- Set three: all the possible English translations (e.g. I must, you must etc.).

Lay all the cards face up on a table and match them up, e.g. *Je + dois +* I must. Do this a couple of times to practise and then time yourself to see how fast you can match them up.

Repeat the same process with the other two remaining modal verbs. Then mix all three sets of pronouns, verbs and English translations up together and see how fast you can match them up. Can you match them all correctly in 30 seconds or faster?

**TOP TIP**

This activity can be repeated by adding more and more verbs to help you learn them, and will really support you in recognising verbs when you are reading.

# Reflexive verbs

The last set of verbs we are going to look at in this section are the reflexive verbs. Reflexive verbs are used to describe an action we do to ourselves. You will know if a verb is reflexive because the verb has 'se' before it in the infinitive form, e.g. *se lever* which translates as 'to get up' or, literally, 'to get oneself up'.

## Exercise 5

Look up the following verbs in a dictionary. Which ones are reflexive?

| | | |
|---|---|---|
| to enjoy yourself | to take | to remember |
| to shave | to sit | to get angry |
| to wake up | to leave | to put on make-up |
| to dance | to bathe | to forget |

The reflexive verbs are formed by adding an extra pronoun when you conjugate them. Here are a few examples. Notice that when the pronouns 'me', 'te' and 'se' are followed by a vowel they become m', t' and s', e.g. *je **m'**amuse, tu **t'**amuses, il **s'**amuse* etc.

| Se réveiller | S'amuser | S'entendre |
|---|---|---|
| je **me** réveille | je **m'**amuse | je **m'**entends |
| tu **te** réveilles | tu **t'**amuses | tu **t'**entends |
| il/elle/on **se** réveille | il/elle/on **s'**amuse | il/elle/on **s'**entend |
| nous **nous** réveillons | nous **nous** amusons | nous **nous** entendons |
| vous **vous** réveillez | vous **vous** amusez | vous **vous** entendez |
| ils/elles **se** réveillent | ils/elles **s'**amusent | ils/elles **s'**entendent |

## Exercise 6

Read the following sentences and fill in the missing pronouns, e.g. *je me couche.*

1. *Il boit trop d'alcool et il ___ soûle souvent. C'est dangereux et il doit ___ en occuper.*
2. *Les gens ___ droguent pour échapper à leurs soucis.*
3. *Les filles ___ maquillent avant de sortir le soir.*
4. *Je ___ amuse quand je ___ promène.*
5. *Nous ____ intéressons beaucoup à la santé et au bien-être.*
6. *Quand est-ce que vous _____ mariez ?*
7. *Est-ce que tu ____ sens obligé d'acheter le dernier modèle de téléphone portable ?*
8. *Je __énerve quand ma mère me demande de recycler. C'est pénible comme tâche.*
9. *On ___ fatigue en faisant du sport.*
10. *Vous _____ empêchez d'apprendre le chinois si vous avez trop peur de parler.*

# Learning in context

In the learning topic, you will reflect on how you learn in Modern Languages. When learning a language, it helps to develop an awareness of how you learn best, as this allows you to remember vocabulary in a way which works for you.

## Talking about modern languages

The first part of the topic focuses on learning in modern languages.

| | |
|---|---|
| *Quand j'apprends le français, je préfère ...* | When I learn French I prefer ... |
| *... écouter* | ... to listen |
| *... parler* | ... to talk |
| *... lire* | ... reading |
| *... écrire* | ... to write |
| *... jouer* | ... to play |
| *... faire des activités de coopération* | ... to do cooperative activities |
| *... travailler en groupe* | ... to work in groups |
| *... travailler avec un partenaire* | ... to work with a partner |
| *... travailler tout(e) seul(e)* | ... working alone |
| *Je suis fort(e) à l'oral* | I'm good at talking |
| *J'ai une bonne mémoire* | I have a good memory |
| *Je trouve que (parler) c'est difficile* | I find it difficult to (speak) |
| *Je me sens _____ quand je parle français* | I feel _____ when I speak French |
| *timide* | shy |
| *nerveux/nerveuse* | nervous |
| *sûr(e) de moi* | sure of myself |

### Exercise 1

Unjumble the following phrases and rewrite them in the correct order.

1. *groupe préfère Je travailler en.*
2. *les J'aime de coopération. activités*
3. *Je parle me de moi sens quand je français. sûr*
4. *fort Je l'écoute. suis à*
5. *pour apprendre. J'aime jouer*

GOT IT? ☐ ☐ ☐

## Exercise 2

Answer the following questions and keep a note of your colours to find out what your learning style is.

1. *Je préfère les cours où ...*

| | | |
|---|---|---|
| *on peut discuter en groupe.* | *on peut faire des activités.* | *on peut regarder des présentations.* |

2. *Pendant que je travaille en classe ...*

| | | |
|---|---|---|
| *je préfère qu'on m'explique comment faire.* | *je tripote quelque chose, je tambourine des doigts sur la table ou je bats la mesure avec le pied.* | *je fais des dessins dans mon cahier.* |

3. *Quand j'apprends quelque chose de nouveau ...*

| | | |
|---|---|---|
| *je chante, je fredonne ou je parle.* | *je préfère me débrouiller tout(e) seul(e).* | *je préfère qu'on me montre comment faire.* |

4. *Si j'ai du temps libre ...*

| | | |
|---|---|---|
| *j'aime écouter de la musique ou parler avec mes amis au téléphone.* | *j'aime sortir pour faire des activités comme jouer au foot par exemple.* | *j'aime regarder un film ou la télévision.* |

5. *En classe, je me déconcentre quand ...*

| | | |
|---|---|---|
| *j'entends quelque chose qui me distrait.* | *je dois rester sans bouger trop longtemps.* | *je vois quelque chose par la fenêtre.* |

Count the colours and check what it says about your learning style below. What three pieces of advice are you given for the types of activities you should do when learning a language?

### TOP TIP

Follow the advice for your learning style to help you revise your French vocabulary.

### Bleu – Vous êtes apprenant visuel
*On vous conseille d'utiliser des diagrammes et des graphique et d'avoir des images à côté du vocabulaire : des petits dessins dans vos listes de vocabulaire, par exemple. Vous pouvez également créer des cartes de vocabulaire (comme des flashcards) et il est important de beaucoup lire !*

### Rose – Vous êtes apprenant auditif
*Vous préférez écouter quand vous apprenez. Ecoutez beaucoup de français, à la radio, regardez beaucoup de clips vidéos (sur YouTube, par exemple) et surtout lisez et écoutez en même temps !*

### Vert – Vous êtes apprenant kinesthésique
*Pour vous, il est important de faire quelque chose pendant que vous apprenez. Les jeux interactifs en ligne vous aideront beaucoup. Prenez des notes pendant que vous lisez ou écoutez. Enfin, répétez souvent du vocabulaire à voix haute et si possible, ajoutez des activités !*

# Learning in other subjects

Now let's look at learning more widely in other subject areas.
What are you good at? Which subjects do you enjoy most?

| | |
|---|---|
| *J'étudie ...* | I study ... |
| *... l'anglais* | ... English |
| *... les maths* | ... maths |
| *... la biologie* | ... biology |
| *... la chimie* | ... chemistry |
| *... la physique* | ... physics |
| *... la géographie* | ... geography |
| *... l'histoire* | ... history |
| *... l'économie domestique* | ... home economics |
| *... les travaux manuels* | ... craft and design |
| *... la musique* | ... music |
| *... le dessin* | ... art |
| *... l'informatique* | ... computing |
| *... l'EPS* | ... PE |

| | |
|---|---|
| *c'est compliqué* | it's complicated |
| *c'est difficile* | it's difficult |
| *c'est intéressant* | it's interesting |
| *c'est facile* | it's easy |
| *c'est ennuyeux* | it's boring |
| *c'est pénible* | it's painful |
| *c'est utile* | it's useful |
| *le (la) prof est compréhensif/ive* | the teacher is understanding |
| *c'est difficile à comprendre* | it's difficult to understand |
| *c'est difficile à suivre* | it's difficult to follow |
| *c'est facile à comprendre* | it's easy to understand |

| | |
|---|---|
| *je préfère les matières (pratiques) comme ...* | I prefer (practical) subjects like ... |
| *les matières créatives ...* | creative subjects ... |
| *les matières logiques ...* | logical subjects ... |
| *les matières scientifiques ...* | scientific subjects ... |
| *je suis plus fort(e) en (maths) qu'en (chimie)* | I'm better in (maths) than in (chemistry) |
| *je suis plus faible en (anglais) qu'en (français)* | I'm weaker in (English) than in (French) |
| *(Le dessin) m'intéresse plus que (les maths)* | (Art) interests me more than (maths) |
| *(L'espagnol) m'intéresse beaucoup* | I'm very interested in (Spanish) |
| *Il y a trop de devoirs* | There is too much homework |
| *J'ai environ _ heures de devoirs par semaine* | I have about __ hours of homework per week |

## Exercise 1

Organise the subjects on the previous page into each of the columns below according to your opinion of them.

| C'est facile | C'est intéressant | C'est utile | C'est compliqué | C'est pénible |
|---|---|---|---|---|
| | | | | |

## Exercise 2

Listen to the following opinions about school subjects and for each one write either *'Je suis d'accord'* (I agree) or *'Je ne suis pas d'accord'* (I don't agree).

## Exercise 3

Now read the text below with a French teenager, Ahmed, giving his opinions about school and learning.

*Selon moi, il est important de pouvoir choisir entre de nombreuses matières à l'école et de pouvoir personnaliser son emploi du temps autant que possible. Cependant, il faut se souvenir qu'il y aura toujours certaines matières obligatoires.*

*Je pense que je suis une personne plutôt créative et je dirais que je suis assez doué en dessin par exemple. À mon avis, je suis plus fort dans les matières créatives comme le dessin, la musique et l'anglais que dans les matières logiques comme les maths ou les sciences. Mais mon père croit que c'est parce que je ne consacre pas assez de temps à faire des maths. C'est vrai que je trouve ça trop compliqué et assez pénible.*

*En général, les matières pratiques comme l'EPS ne m'intéressent pas vraiment mais elles me plaisent parce qu'elles font reposer le cerveau !*

*Pour ma part, je n'ai aucune envie de faire mes devoirs le soir mais je sais, pourtant, que je n'ai pas le choix et que c'est très important de les faire si on veut réussir. Je suis assez faible en histoire, donc je dois faire beaucoup de devoirs pour arriver à avoir de bonnes notes.*

1. What does Ahmed say about art? (1)
2. What does Ahmed's dad think about his approach to maths? (1)
3. What does Ahmed say about practical subjects? (2)
4. What is his attitude to homework? (3)
5. What does he say about history? (2)
6. What is Ahmed's attitude overall to subject choice? Tick the correct box. (1)

| | | |
|---|---|---|
| 1. | It's important to have choice but there are some subjects you just have to do. | ☐ |
| 2. | He thinks you should just do what you are interested in. | ☐ |
| 3. | He thinks you should choose according to the career you want. | ☐ |

**TOP TIP**

Go through the text from Exercise 1 and pick out the opinion phrases. Copy them into a list and keep them as a bank of useful opinion phrases that you can use again.

# Preparing for exams

The final part of the learning topic looks at preparing for exams, just as you are now! It can be a useful process to reflect on how you study and what works best for you.

| | |
|---|---|
| *Pour préparer mes examens* | To prepare for exams |
| *je fais des révisions* | I revise |
| *je lis mes notes* | I read my notes |
| *je consulte des annales* | I do past papers |
| *j'établis des horaires de révisions* | I make a revision timetable |
| *je vais aux cours de révisions* | I go to revision classes |
| *je prends des cours particuliers* | I get after-school tuition |
| *j'étudie avec mes amis* | I study with my friends |
| *j'étudie tout(e) seul(e)* | I study alone |
| *j'étudie chez moi ...* | I study at home ... |
| *dans ma chambre* | in my bedroom |
| *dans la cuisine* | in the kitchen |
| *dans le salon* | in the living room |
| *je préfère travailler le soir/le matin* | I prefer to work in the evening/in the morning |
| *je regarde la télé quand j'étudie* | I watch TV when I'm studying |
| *j'écoute la radio* | I listen to the radio |
| *j'écoute de la musique* | I listen to music |
| *j'arrive à me concentrer plus facilement quand j'écoute de la musique* | I can concentrate more easily when I listen to music |
| *je dois me concentrer sur mes études* | I have to concentrate on my studies |
| *je me déconcentre facilement* | I lose my concentration easily |

## Exercise 1

Listen to the following conversation between Jean and Sara about study habits and fill in the missing information.

**Sara :** *Tu as des examens bientôt, Jean ?*
**Jean :** *Oui, c'est l'horreur, j'ai __1__ à faire !*
**Sara :** *Tu as des examens en quelles matières ?*
**Jean :** *J'ai des examens en __2__.*
**Sara :** *Et un examen en français aussi ?*
**Jean :** *Oui, j'ai oublié ! Un examen en français aussi ! Ça fait six matières au total ! C'est trop !*
**Sara :** *Et comment est-ce que tu révises ?*
**Jean :** *D'abord, __3__ et puis j'essaie de m'y atteler.*
**Sara :** *Tu fais combien d'heures par jour ?*
**Jean :** *En général, je fais environ __4__. Je fais __5__, __6__ et __7__.*
**Sara :** *C'est beaucoup! Tu n'es pas fatigué ?*
**Jean :** *Si, et __8__ mais __9__ et __10__, donc il faut que __11__.*
**Sara :** *Tu préfères travailler le matin ou le soir ?*
**Jean :** *__12__ mais à mon avis, les deux sont pénibles !*
**Sara :** *Est-ce-que tu écoutes de la musique pendant que tu travailles ?*
**Jean :** *__13__ quand je travaille. __14__ et les révisions sont plus amusantes lorsqu'on en écoute !*
**Sara :** *C'est vrai ! OK, je te laisse travailler ! Bonne chance, Jean, bon courage !*
**Jean :** *Merci, Sara ! C'est gentil.*

### TOP TIP

When learning vocabulary, skim-read word lists or texts and highlight the phrases you don't understand. Focus your attention on remembering them.

## Exercise 2

Using the vocabulary on page 52 to help you, translate the following revision advice into French.

1. To prepare for my exams, I read my notes and do past papers.
2. I prefer to work alone.
3. I study with my friends at my house.
4. I never watch TV when I study.
5. I prefer to study at night.

# Education

This topic focuses on the broader subject of education and how education systems in France differ from our own.

## Comparing education systems

This part of the topic compares Scottish school life with school life in France. How do they compare in your opinion? Does one seem better than the other?

| | |
|---|---|
| *Le lycée commence à __ heures et finit à __ heures.* | School starts at __ o'clock and finishes at __ o'clock. |
| *Il y a des cours du lundi au vendredi.* | There are lessons from Monday till Friday. |
| *Il n'y a pas de cours le vendredi après-midi.* | There are no lessons on Friday afternoons. |
| *Il n'y a pas de cours le week-end.* | There are no lessons at the weekend. |
| *Il y a __ cours le matin et __ cours l'après-midi.* | There are __ lessons in the morning and __ lessons in the afternoon. |
| *Il y a une pause de midi à __ heures.* | There is a lunch break at __ o'clock. |
| *La pause de midi dure __ heure(s).* | The lunch lasts __ hour(s). |
| *Il y a une récréation le matin à __ heures.* | There is a break in the morning at __ o'clock. |
| *La récréation dure __ minutes.* | The break lasts __ minutes. |
| *Les grandes vacances durent ...* | The summer holidays last ... |

### Exercise 1

Use the vocabulary above to write seven sentences describing your school life.

### Exercise 2

Read the text about school life in France and then, using the text to help you, answer the questions in French below.

*Chie :* En France, au lycée, il y a des cours du lundi au vendredi. Le mercredi après-midi est libre pour faire du sport, des cours de musique ou des devoirs. La journée scolaire commence à huit heures et demie et finit à seize heures trente. Il y a une récréation le matin à 11 heures moins le quart qui dure quinze minutes. Puis nous avons une pause déjeuner entre midi et quatorze heures, qui dure deux heures au total. Normalement, je mange à la cantine avec mes amis.

Il y a quatre cours le matin et deux cours l'après-midi, et chaque cours dure environ une heure.

En ce qui concerne les vacances, il y a une longue pause pendant l'été et les grandes vacances durent deux mois ! C'est extra, j'adore les vacances !

**Questions:**

*Quels sont les jours d'école ?*
*Quels jours sont libres ?*
*La journée scolaire commence à quelle heure ?*
*La journée scolaire finit à quelle heure ?*
*La récréation est à quelle heure ?*
*Ça dure combien de temps ?*
*Il y a une pause déjeuner ?*
*Tu manges où normalement ?*
*Combien as-tu de cours le matin ?*
*Combien as-tu de cours l'après-midi ?*
*Les grandes vacances durent combien de temps ?*

### TOP TIP

Treat all reading texts as a source of new phrases you can use in your own writing and speaking. Keep a list of phrases you think you would like to use so that you can refer back to it at a later date.

## Exercise 3

Now look at the diagram below, which shows us the difference between the Scottish and French school systems.

| Age | 11–12 | 12–13 | 13–14 | 14–15 | Brevet | 15–16 | 16–17 | 17–18 | Bac (ou baccalauréat) |
|---|---|---|---|---|---|---|---|---|---|
| France | Collège | | | | | Lycée | | | |
| | Sixième (6ème) | Cinquième (5ème) | Quatrième (4ème) | Troisième (3ème) | | Seconde | Première | Terminale | |
| Ecosse | Ecole primaire | Collège | | | Fin de Broad General Education | National Qualifications | | | |
| | | | | | | Senior Phase | | | |
| | P7 | S1 | S2 | S3 | | S4 | S5 | S6 | |

Using the information provided in the table above, complete the sentences below with the missing information.

1. *En France, on commence le lycée à partir de l'âge de ____ ans.*
2. *Entre l'âge de 11 et 15 ans, on va au _____.*
3. *On passe un examen qui s'appelle le brevet à la fin du _____.*
4. *La dernière année de lycée s'appelle la _____.*
5. *Avant de terminer ses études, il faut réussir un examen qui s'appelle _____.*

# Learner responsibilities

As a learner, what responsibilities do you have within your own education? Knowing this and working towards these goals is a key part of achieving success in your studies.

| | |
|---|---|
| *Je dois (suivre les règles)* | I must (follow the rules) |
| *J'essaie toujours de (faire mes devoirs)* | I try always to (do my homework) |
| *Un bon élève doit (faire ses devoirs)* | A good pupil must (do their homework) |
| *écouter le professeur* | listen to the teacher |
| *travailler dur* | work hard |
| *faire des révisions* | revise |
| *respecter les autres* | respect others |
| *être bien préparé* | be well-prepared |
| *être bien organisé* | be well-organised |
| *être autonome dans son travail* | be self-reliant in their work |
| *bien se comporter* | behave well |
| *Un bon prof doit (écouter ses élèves)* | A good teacher should (listen to their pupils) |
| *être compréhensif* | be understanding |
| *être patient* | be patient |
| *essayer des approches différentes* | try different approaches |
| *vous laisser le temps de réflechir* | leave you time to think |
| *avoir le sens de l'humour* | have a sense of humour |

**Grammar blast!**

## devoir

The verb *'devoir'* means 'to have to'. Let's look at how this verb is formed in the present tense. It's a useful verb that comes up often, so it's worth knowing.

**TOP TIP**

Create your own success criteria list and use it to check all of your writing. It could include spelling, accents, gender, adjective agreements, verb endings and tenses.

| *devoir* (to have to) | | | |
|---|---|---|---|
| *je dois* | I have to | *nous devons* | we have to |
| *tu dois* | you have to | *vous devez* | you have to |
| *il/elle doit* | he/she has to | *ils/elles doivent* | they have to |
| *on doit* | one has to<br>we have to | | |

### Exercise 1

Using the vocabulary opposite, write five sentences describing what you think makes '*un bon élève*' and '*un bon prof*'.

### Exercise 2

Take the following text and complete it so that it takes the correct form of devoir in all the gaps.

*Nous __1__ bien travailler au lycée parce que c'est important pour nos futurs carrières et personnellement, je __2__ réussir mes examens. Mes camarades de classe sont un peu bruyants parfois et à mon avis, ils __3__ mieux se comporter. Sinon, ça nous distrait tous. Cependant, le professeur __4__ également faire quelque chose et c'est sa responsabilité d'avoir une classe qui travaille bien. Nous __5__ toujours écouter et respecter les professeurs.*

### Exercise 3

Listen to the following school pupils talking about their attitude in class. Decide if they are a '*bon élève*' or a '*mauvais élève*' and then give two reasons why for each.

| | **Bon élève ?** | **Mauvais élève ?** | **Pourquoi ?** |
|---|---|---|---|
| 1. Lucas<br>2. Alain<br>3. Jennie | | | |

### Exercise 4

What are your qualities as a learner? Write 30–50 words in French about what you consider your qualities to be. These can then be used as part of your job application writing task in the final writing assessment. The vocabulary below may help you.

| | |
|---|---|
| *Je me considère comme un bon élève parce que ...* | I consider myself to be a good pupil because ... |
| *Je préfère bien me comporter* | I prefer to behave |
| *J'essaie de bien me comporter* | I try to behave |
| *Il ne faut pas déranger les autres* | You mustn't disturb others |
| *Je n'arrive pas à me concentrer et à parler en même temps* | I can't concentrate and talk at the same time |

# Employability

The employability topic looks at the world of work and your future plans. Remember that languages on your CV is something that stands out to employers and can complement any career choice.

## Jobs

Now let's look at part-time jobs and how these fit in with your studies and life.

| | |
|---|---|
| J'ai un petit boulot | I have a part-time job |
| Je travaille dans | I work in |
| ... un supermarché | ... a supermarket |
| ... un café | ... a cafe |
| ... un magasin | ... a shop |
| Je fais du baby-sitting | I babysit |
| Je gagne __ livres par heure | I earn __ pounds an hour |
| C'est bien payé | It's well paid |
| Ce n'est pas bien payé | It's not well paid |
| Je réponds au téléphone | I answer the phone |
| Je sers les clients | I serve the customers |
| Je travaille le samedi et le mardi après l'école | I work on Saturdays and Tuesdays after school |
| Je commence le travail à neuf heures | I start work at 9.00 |
| Je finis le travail à dix-sept heures | I finish work at 17.00 |
| Il y a trop de travail à faire | There's too much work to do |
| C'est monotone | It's monotonous |
| C'est une bonne expérience | It's good experience |
| Le patron est (sympa) | The boss is (nice) |

### Exercise 1

Read the following text about working part time and then see if you can find the French for the phrases that are listed below.

*J'ai un petit boulot dans un café près de chez moi. Je travaille le week-end, donc, le samedi et le dimanche. En général, je travaille pendant la journée mais des fois, je dois aussi travailler le vendredi soir. C'est embêtant mais je n'ai pas le choix. Normalement, je m'occupe des clients et je prépare des boissons, comme par exemple des cafés et des thés. Ce n'est pas bien payé mais comme c'est un café, je gagne aussi des pourboires. Le patron du café est gentil mais le chef, qui fait toute la cuisine, est toujours stressé et de mauvaise humeur quand il travaille. J'évite d'aller trop souvent dans la cuisine ! Il me fait un peu peur !*

1. I work the weekend
2. during the day
3. I've no choice
4. I look after the customers
5. I also earn tips
6. I avoid going
7. He frightens me a bit

## Exercise 2

Listen to the following people talking about their jobs and complete the table below.

|  | **1.  Angela** | **2.  Guilhem** |
|---|---|---|
| Job<br>Days of work<br>Start time<br>Finish time<br>Duties<br>Pay<br>Opinion |  |  |

## Exercise 3

Match the sentence starters with the correct endings.

| | | | |
|---|---|---|---|
| 1. | *J'ai un petit boulot* | a. | *les clients.* |
| 2. | *Il y a toujours trop de* | b. | *assez d'argent.* |
| 3. | *Je ne gagne pas* | c. | *du nettoyage.* |
| 4. | *Je gagne environ* | d. | *dans une boulangerie.* |
| 5. | *C'est monotone mais* | e. | *c'est une bonne expérience.* |
| 6. | *Je sers* | f. | *travail à faire.* |
| 7. | *Je fais* | g. | *sept heures du matin et cinq heures du soir.* |
| 8. | *Je travaille entre* | h. | *cinq euros de l'heure.* |
| 9. | *Je travaille le week-end* | i. | *à la fin de la journée.* |
| 10. | *Je suis souvent très fatigué* | j. | *et le mardi après l'école.* |

## Exercise 4

Now rewrite the phrases from Exercise 3 and put them into what you consider to be the correct order. You can also add linking words and opinion phrases to make your writing flow more. A few examples are given for you below. There is a sample text for you in the answers section.

| | |
|---|---|
| *et* | and |
| *mais* | but |
| *normalement* | normally |
| *d'habitude* | usually |
| *cependant* | however |
| *pourtant* | however |
| *alors* | so |
| *à mon avis* | in my opinion |
| *selon moi* | according to me |

# Future plans

This next section will focus on future plans and how you then form the future tense.

| | |
|---|---|
| à l'avenir | in the future |
| je continuerai mes études | I will continue my studies |
| je passerai mes examens | I will sit my exams |
| j'irai à la fac | I will go to university |
| j'étudierai (les sciences) | I will study (science) |
| je passerai un diplôme | I will do a degree |
| je travaillerai | I will work |
|   dans l'informatique |   in computing |
|   dans le commerce |   in business |
|   à l'étranger |   abroad |
| je travaillerai comme (ingénieur) | I will work as (an engineer) |
| je quitterai l'école ... | I will leave school ... |
|   ... l'année prochaine |   ... next year |
|   ... dans trois ans |   ... in three years |
| je voyagerai | I will go travelling |
| je prendrai une année sabbatique | I will take a gap year |
| je ferai du bénévolat (en Afrique) | I will volunteer (in Africa) |
| je ferai le tour du monde | I will go around the world |

**Grammar blast!**

### The future tense

The future tense is formed by using a future stem of the verb (this is usually the infinitive) and the following endings.

| travailler (to work) | | | |
|---|---|---|---|
| je travaille**rai** | I will work | nous travaille**rons** | we will work |
| tu travaille**ras** | you will work | vous travaille**rez** | you will work |
| il/elle travaille**ra** | he will work | ils/elles travaille**ront** | they will work |
| on travaille**ra** | one will work<br>we will work | | |

Note that the common irregular verb endings are:

| Verb | Future stem | Example |
|---|---|---|
| aller | ir | j'irai (I will go) |
| faire | fer | tu feras (you will do) |
| être | ser | nous serons (we will be) |
| avoir | aur | vous aurez (you will have) |

Using the vocabulary opposite to help you, complete the sentences below to describe your own future plans.

1. *L'année prochaine ...*
2. *Dans deux ans ...*
3. *Dans trois ans ...*
4. *Dans cinq ans ...*
5. *Dans dix ans ...*

Choose one word from each column to make up six sentences in French and then translate them into English. A couple of examples are done for you below:

1. *J'irai en Europe* (remember *je* becomes *j'* when followed by a vowel).
2. *Je gagnerai beaucoup d'argent.*

> ### TOP TIP
> You can also express things in the future by using the immediate future tense using aller + infinitive, which translates as 'going to'. E.g. *Je vais étudier* – I am going to study.

| Pronouns | Future stems | Verb endings | Sentence endings |
|----------|--------------|--------------|------------------|
| *je* | *gagner* | *ai* | *un emploi* |
| *tu* | *travailler* | *as* | *en Europe* |
| *il* | *continuer* | *a* | *à étudier* |
| *elle* | *ir* | *ons* | *en France* |
| *on* | *voyager* | *ez* | *beaucoup d'argent* |
| *nous*<br>*vous*<br>*ils*<br>*elles* | *ser*<br>*aur*<br>*chercher*<br>*achèter*<br>*vivr* | *ont* | *à l'université*<br>*dans (les médias)*<br>*comme (médecin)*<br>*une voiture*<br>*(dans) un appartement* |

Now read the following text and highlight all the examples of the future tense. There are 25 altogether.

Then select those that apply to your future.
*J'ai beaucoup de projets d'avenir passionnants ! L'année prochaine, je passerai mon bac et avec un peu de chance et beaucoup de travail, je serai reçue et je quitterai le lycée. Je n'irai pas à la fac tout de suite parce que je prendrai une année sabbatique pour voyager avec ma meilleure amie, Amandine. Nous ferons du bénévolat pendant six mois dans une école en Amérique du Sud. Nous enseignerons et nous aiderons les enfants à apprendre le français. Quand j'y serai, j'apprendrai l'espagnol et ça m'aidera beaucoup dans ma future carrière. Après, nous voyagerons en Amérique du Sud : nous visiterons le Brésil, l'Argentine et le Chili. J'aurai beaucoup d'expériences culturelles passionnantes à partager ! Une fois rentrée en France, j'irai à l'université à Paris où j'étudierai l'espagnol, l'allemand et le marketing. Je louerai un appartement avec des amis et je serai très contente d'avoir mon indépendance ! Après la fac, je trouverai un bon emploi, bien payé et je vivrai peut-être à l'étranger. J'habiterai à Londres, Madrid ou Berlin sans problème. Je gagnerai beaucoup d'argent, j'achèterai une belle maison et je prendrai plein de vacances dans des pays exotiques ! Mon avenir sera fantastique !*

# Work and CVs

What did you plan to do during your work experience? How was it? Did you have a good or bad experience? This topic will explore ways you can discuss both your planning and your evaluation of this in French.

## Planning for work experience

Let's look first of all at planning for work experience. To do this, we'll use the immediate future tense.

| | |
|---|---|
| *Je vais faire un stage ...* | I'm going to do work experience ... |
| *... au centre sportif* | ... at the sport centre |
| *... dans un bureau* | ... in an office |
| *... chez un avocat* | ... at a lawyer's |
| *Ça va durer une semaine* | It's going to be for a week |
| *Je vais y aller ...* | I'm going to go ... |
| *... à pied* | ... on foot |
| *... en bus* | ... by bus |
| *Je vais porter (un costume)* | I'm going to wear (a suit) |
| *Je vais manger (à la cantine)* | I'm going to eat (at the canteen) |
| *Je me sens (nerveux/euse)* | I feel (nervous) |

**Grammar blast!**

### The immediate future

The immediate future refers to things which are going to happen. In order to form the immediate future, it's just a case of using **aller + the infinitive** of the verb. For example, *Nous allons manger* – We are going to eat.

The verb *aller* is conjugated as below:

| *aller* (to go) | | | |
|---|---|---|---|
| *je vais* | I go | *nous allons* | we go |
| *tu vas* | you go | *vous allez* | you go |
| *il/elle va* | he/she goes | *ils/elles vont* | they go |
| *on va* | one goes/we go | | |

## Exercise 1

Translate the following sentences in the immediate future from French into English.

1. *Je vais classer des papiers.*
2. *Je vais me lever à huit heures du matin.*
3. *Nous allons répondre au téléphone.*
4. *Tu vas travailler au contact des clients.*
5. *Ils vont beaucoup apprendre.*

## Exercise 2

Using the immediate future tense, answer the following questions about planning for work experience. The first one is done for you. You will also find sample responses in the answers section.

1. *Où est-ce que tu vas travailler ? Je vais travailler (dans un garage).*
2. *Tu vas te lever à quelle heure ?*
3. *Comment est-ce que tu vas aller au travail ?*
4. *Qu'est-ce que tu vas faire au travail ?*

## Exercise 3

Reorder the following questions and answers about work experience between a teacher and a student so that they make a complete conversation. Listen once you've reordered them to check your answers.

### Professeur
- *Alors Caty, qu'est-ce que tu vas faire comme stage ?*
- *Ah, c'est beaucoup de responsabilité ! Où est-ce que tu vas travailler ?*
- *Ah bon, c'est très bien ! Et qu'est-ce que tu vas faire au travail ?*
- *Tu vas commencer à quelle heure ?*
- *Alors je te souhaite bon courage et bonne chance !*
- *Qu'est-ce que tu vas porter au travail ?*
- *Comment est-ce que tu vas aller au travail ?*

### Elève
- *Je vais commencer à huit heures et quart. C'est un peu trop tôt pour moi !*
- *En fait, le cabinet médical n'est pas trop loin de chez moi, donc je vais y aller à pied.*
- *Merci, monsieur !*
- *Je vais classer les dossiers des patients.*
- *Oui, mais je suis une personne très responsable quand même ! Je vais travailler au centre-ville.*
- *Je vais travailler chez un médecin.*
- *A mon avis, il est important d'être bien habillé, donc je vais porter une jupe et un chemisier.*

**TOP TIP**

If you want to make the immediate future negative, all you need to do is add **ne** and **pas** around the parts of *aller*, e.g. Je **ne** vais **pas** travailler – I am not going to work. *Facile* !

# Reviewing your work experience

Now let's look at how you would describe a work experience that you have completed. In order to do this you now need to use the past tense, the perfect tense and the imperfect tense.

| Mon stage en entreprise | My work experience |
|---|---|
| C'était comment ? | How was it? |
| C'était ... | It was ... |
| ... une expérience intéressante | ... an interesting experience |
| ... facile/long/dur/varié | ... easy/long/hard/varied |
| J'ai travaillé comme sécrétaire | I worked as a secretary |
| J'ai classé des documents | I filed documents |
| Je suis allé(e) au travail (à vélo) | I went to work (by bike) |
| J'ai appris comment (parler aux clients) | I learned how to (speak to customers) |
| J'ai dû répondre au téléphone | I had to answer the phone |
| Je ne me suis pas amusé(e) | I didn't enjoy it |
| Le stage a duré quinze jours | The placement lasted a fortnight |
| J'avais peur | I was scared |
| J'étais nerveux/nerveuse | I was nervous |
| Je m'entendais bien avec mes collègues | I got on well with my workmates |
| Le stage m'a préparé(e) au monde du travail | Work experience prepared me for the world of work |

## Exercise 1

Match the correct sentence starters with the endings. Write the sentences out in full.

| | | | |
|---|---|---|---|
| 1. | Mon stage | a. | au travail en bus. |
| 2. | J'ai appris | b. | une tenue élégante. |
| 3. | Le stage a duré | c. | durait une heure. |
| 4. | Je m'entendais bien | d. | comment discuter avec les clients au téléphone. |
| 5. | Je suis allé | e. | le travail à neuf heures. |
| 6. | J'ai porté | f. | une semaine. |
| 7. | Je commençais | g. | au travail. |
| 8. | La pause déjeuner | h. | a été une expérience intéressante et variée. |
| 9. | Je me suis amusé(e) | i. | à dix-sept heures. |
| 10. | Je finissais | j. | avec mes collègues. |

### The perfect tense – *le passé composé*

The perfect tense (*'le passé composé'* in French) is used to describe completed actions in the past. It is made up of two parts: either one of the verbs *'avoir'* or *'être'* (which is called the auxiliary or helper verb) followed by the **past participle** of the verb, e.g. *Je suis allé(e)*. The table below shows how it is constructed. You will find a full explanation on the perfect tense in the **Focus on grammar** section on page 91.

**Auxilliary verb + Past participle = Perfect tense**

| Auxiliary verb | + | Past participle | = | Perfect tense | English |
|---|---|---|---|---|---|
| *Je suis* | | *allé(e)* | | *Je suis allé(e)* | I went |
| *J'ai* | | *mangé* | | *J'ai mangé* | I ate |

The vast majority of verbs take *'avoir'* as the auxiliary verb. Reflexive verbs and a group of another 13 verbs take *'être'*. Verbs which take *'être'* have to agree with their subject, e.g. *elle est arrivée* and *elles sont arrivées*. So if you're a girl you would write *je suis arrivée*, adding the extra 'e' to make it feminine.

You will find detailed information about the perfect tense and *être* verbs on page 93.

#### Exercise 2

Now using the perfect tense constructions from the table below, write 10 sentences in the perfect tense, adding the sentence endings provided. Hint: where there are letters in brackets, these verbs will take *être* as the auxiliary and will take the extra **e** if you're a girl.

| | | | | |
|---|---|---|---|---|
| *j'ai fini* | *j'ai joué* | *j'ai porté* | *je suis allé(e)* | *j'ai mangé* |
| *j'ai ouvert* | *j'ai travaillé* | *j'ai gagné* | *je suis arrivé(e)* | *j'ai dû* |

1. *dans un office de tourisme.*
2. *à cinq heures moins le quart.*
3. *les lettres des clients.*
4. *aux cartes avec les patients.*
5. *une tenue de sport.*
6. *au travail en voiture.*
7. *toujours à l'heure.*
8. *au café avec mes amis pendant la pause de midi.*
9. *ranger les rayons.*
10. *environ cinq euros cinquante de l'heure.*

### TOP TIP

Create a short sentence in the perfect tense and use it for future reference as a guide on how to form it, e.g. 'J'ai joué au foot et je suis allé(e) au cinéma le week-end'. The sentence tells us it's complete and gives us an example with both être and avoir !

#### Exercise 3

Now go back through the sentences from the previous task and add at least two opinions for each one using **C'était**.

E.g *J'ai dû ranger les rayons. C'était pénible et fatigant.*

# Reviewing successes

In this final part of the topic, we'll bring together what you've learned about using the future, immediate future and past tenses to talk about what you've achieved, what your ambitions are and how you would discuss these when applying for a job. This will also support you in preparing for the writing part of the exam.

| | |
|---|---|
| date/lieu de naissance | date/place of birth |
| compétences | skills |
| intérêts | interests |
| expériences professionelles | professional experiences |
| stage professionnel | work experience |
| une référence | a reference |

## Exercise 1

Look at the qualities below and decide if they would make a 'bon candidat' or a 'mauvais candidat' for a job.

| | |
|---|---|
| Je suis toujours à l'heure | Je suis une personne très responsable |
| Je suis toujours en retard | Je suis travailleur/euse |
| J'ai un bon relationnel | J'ai un mauvais relationnel |
| Je suis paresseux/euse | Je suis irresponsable |

## Exercise 2

Look at the example of a CV template below. Read the letter that follows and complete the CV for Zuri using the information provided.

Nom

Prénom

Adresse

Date de naissance

Lieu de naissance

Nationalité(s)

Matières étudiées au lycée

Expériences professionelles

Compétences linguistiques

Qualités personnelles

Centres d'intérêt

Zuri Fernandez
7 rue de la grande plage
64200 BIARRITZ
France

Biarritz, le 5 juin 2014

Cher Monsieur, chère Madame,
Suite à votre annonce, je me permets de poser ma candidature pour le poste de réceptionniste dans votre hôtel.

J'ai la double nationalité car mes parents sont d'origine espagnole mais je suis née et j'ai grandi en France. Par conséquent, je parle l'espagnol et le français couramment et je parle aussi l'anglais (j'ai un niveau intermédiaire). J'adore apprendre les langues ; d'ailleurs, j'apprends le chinois en ce moment. Cependant, je ne suis actuellement qu'au niveau débutant.

Je suis née le 13 juin 2000 à Biarritz en France et j'y ai habité toute ma vie donc je connais très bien la région, ce qui est important pour renseigner les touristes, je crois!

Au lycée, je suis en seconde et j'ai obtenu mon brevet l'année dernière. Maintenant, j'étudie le français, la géographie, les maths, l'anglais et la musique.

Je dirais que je suis une personne responsable, fiable, raisonnable, chaleureuse et très sociable. Je trouve qu'il est très facile de se faire de nouveaux amis et de parler avec des personnes de cultures et de milieux différents.

L'année dernière, j'ai fait un stage en tant que réceptionniste dans un hôtel ici, à Biarritz, et cela m'a beaucoup plu. J'ai dû accueillir les clients, prendre des réservations et répondre au téléphone. C'était intéressant et j'ai eu l'occasion de pouvoir parler l'anglais, l'espagnol et un peu de chinois aussi!

Sinon, quand je ne travaille pas, je suis très sportive: j'aime les sports nautiques et la danse.

En espérant que ma candidature retiendra votre attention, je vous prie d'agréer, cher Monsieur, chère Madame, l'expression de mes sentiments distingués.

Cordialement,
Zuri Fernandez

Now use the example you've written for Zuri to make up your own CV in French. Look back through your notes and through the rest of this book to help you.

**TOP TIP**

When you are writing a letter in French, you need to ensure that you keep it very formal and use **vous** at all times.

**Exercise 3**

Now try writing your own job application letter. Make sure you include:

- A clear start and finish (including your address and the date)
- Your language skills and what you've studied at school
- Your professional experience (work experience for example)
- Your hobbies and personal qualities
- What you would like to do in the future.

# Focus on grammar: the future tense and the conditional tense

Let's look at the two ways of expressing the future in French: the future tense and the conditional tense.

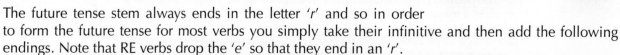

## Future tense

The future tense is the equivalent of will + infinitive in English. For example, I will do, you will do, he will do, etc.

The future tense stem always ends in the letter 'r' and so in order to form the future tense for most verbs you simply take their infinitive and then add the following endings. Note that RE verbs drop the 'e' so that they end in an 'r'.

| *travailler* (to work) | | | |
|---|---|---|---|
| *je travaillerai* | I will work | *nous travaillerons* | we will work |
| *tu travailleras* | you will work | *vous travaillerez* | you will work |
| *il/elle travaillera* | he/she will work | *ils/elles travailleront* | they will work |
| *on travaillera* | one/we will work | | |
| *finir* (to finish) | | | |
| *Je finirai* | I will finish | *nous finirons* | we will finish |
| *tu finiras* | you will finish | *vous finirez* | you will finish |
| *il/elle finira* | he/she will finish | *ils/elles finiront* | they will finish |
| *on finira* | one/we will finish | | |
| *prendre* (to take) | | | |
| *je prendrai* | I will take | *nous prendrons* | we will take |
| *tu prendras* | you will take | *vous prendrez* | you will take |
| *il/elle prendra* | he/she will take | *ils/elles prendront* | they will take |
| *on prendra* | one/we will take | | |

### Exercise 1

Translate the following phrases into French.

1. I will work
2. You will sleep
3. He will travel
4. She will eat
5. We will learn
6. You will write
7. They (f) will learn
8. They (m) will open

Now add to these examples of the future tense to turn them into complete sentences, e.g. '*J'ouvrirai des lettres.*'

There are about 24 irregular future stems in French. Some of the most common verbs are listed in the following table.

Complete the table by adding an example conjugation in the future and the English translation of what it means.

| Infinitive | Stem | Example | Translation |
|---|---|---|---|
| acheter | achèter | j'achèterai | I will buy |
| aller | ir | | |
| avoir | aur | | |
| devoir | devr | | |
| essayer | essayer or essaier | | |
| être | ser | | |
| faire | fer | | |
| falloir | faudr | il faudra | I/you/he/she etc. will have to* |
| pouvoir | pourr | | |
| savoir | saur | | |
| tenir | tiendr | | |
| valoir | vaudr | | |
| voir | verr | | |
| vouloir | voudr | | |

*'*Il faudra*' is the future tense of '*il faut*' and works in the same way, e.g. '*il faudra travailler*' = 'one will have to work'.

**TOP TIP**

The same verbs are irregular in the conditional as well and follow exactly the same rules. Two tenses for the price of one!

**TOP TIP**

If a longer verb contains one of the verbs above (e.g. *maintenir* – to maintain – contains *tenir*) then it will follow the same irregular rules, e.g. '*Je maintiendrai*'.

## The conditional tense

The conditional tense is used to describe future events that might happen. It can be translated as would + infinitive in English, e.g. I would be, I would go, I would travel, etc.

Once you've learned the future tense, forming the conditional tense is easy! It's simply a case of taking the future stems and adding the following conditional endings.

| être | aller | voyager |
|---|---|---|
| Je ser**ais** | J'ir**ais** | Je voyager**ais** |
| Tu ser**ais** | Tu ir**ais** | Tu voyager**ais** |
| Il/elle/on ser**ait** | Il/elle/on ir**ait** | Il/elle/on voyager**ait** |
| Nous ser**ions** | Nous ir**ions** | Nous voyager**ions** |
| Vous ser**iez** | Vous ir**iez** | Vous voyager**iez** |
| Ils/elles ser**aient** | Ils/elles ir**aient** | Ils/elles voyager**aient** |

**TOP TIP**

Do you recognise the conditional endings? They're exactly the same as the imperfect ones!

## Exercise 3

Read the following text by Stéphan, a French Terminale student, and highlight all of the future tense phrases in blue and all of the conditional tense phrases in red.

*Je quitterai le lycée l'année prochaine et j'irai à la fac à Grenoble pour faire des études d'ingénieur et de langues. Je voudrais étudier plusieurs langues, comme l'arabe et le chinois, mais je pense que je n'aurai pas assez de temps pour tout faire ! Je louerai un appartement avec des amis qui seront dans la même université que moi, et j'aimerais vivre pas trop loin du centre-ville comme ça nous serons près de la vie nocturne et des magasins ! Moi et mes amis n'aurons pas beaucoup d'argent, il nous faudra donc un appartement pas cher. Je pourrais payer davantage si je trouvais un petit boulot, mais je préférerais ne pas travailler les week-ends pour me détendre ! Ça serait l'idéal !*

# Planning a trip

This topic looks at holidays: both planning for holidays and talking about past holidays. This will give you more opportunities to practise your past and future tenses.

## Planning a trip

Let's look first of all at making plans for future trips.

| | |
|---|---|
| *Je voudrais aller ...* | I would like to go ... |
| *... en France* | ... to France |
| *... en Espagne* | ... to Spain |
| *... en Allemagne* | ... to Germany |
| *... au Canada* | ... to Canada |
| *... aux Etats-Unis* | ... to the USA |
| *Je voudrais visiter ...* | I would like to visit ... |
| *... les monuments historiques* | ... the historic monuments |
| *... les sites touristiques* | ... the tourist sites |
| *... un parc d'attractions* | ... a theme park |
| *... les magasins* | ... the shops |
| *Je voudrais voir les paysages* | I would like to see the scenery |
| *J'aime voyager parce que ...* | I like to travel because ... |
| *... c'est reposant* | ... it's relaxing |
| *... c'est intéressant* | ... it's interesting |
| *... on peut découvrir d'autres cultures* | ... we can discover different cultures |
| *... on peut goûter de nouvelles cuisines* | ... we can try different food |
| *... on peut rencontrer des gens* | ... we can meet new people |
| *... on peut voir le monde* | ... we can see the world |
| *... on peut parler la langue du pays* | ... we can speak the local language |
| *... on peut élargir ses horizons* | ... we can broadens our horizons |

### Exercise 1

Where would you like to visit? Choose a country to visit, find out what it is in French (remember to check if it's masculine, feminine or plural) and then use the vocabulary above to write about where you would like to go and why.

## TOP TIP

Most country names in French are feminine, but the general rule is that if the name ends in the letter 'e' in French, then it's feminine, e.g. *La France, L'Ecosse, L'Espagne.* There are some exceptions though, so always double-check first!

**Grammar blast!**

### Prepositions and places

Prepositions are words that tell us where something is. Some examples are 'in', 'on top of', 'underneath', etc. When talking about countries and towns, use the following table to help you say 'to' or 'in' a place.

| Place | Masculine | Feminine | Plural |
|---|---|---|---|
| **Countries** | *au* | *en* | *aux* |
| | e.g. *Je vais au Portugal.* | e.g. *Je vais en France.* | e.g. *Je vais aux Pays-Bas.* |
| **Towns** | With towns we always use à, e.g. *Je vais à Glasgow.* | | |

### Exercise 2

The French actress Michelle Ecarlate, star of a detective programme called *Point Rouge*, is going to be filming on location in New York. She is known for being a real diva and is very demanding when going on trips.

Read Michelle Ecarlate's demands and complete this sample trip itinerary for her. She would like to do a cultural activity on every day of her trip.

*Moyen de transport*

*Classe*

*Hôtel*

*Lundi*

*Mardi*

*Mercredi*

*Jeudi*

*Vendredi*

*Samedi*

*Dimanche*

Je suis une personne très chic et il est très important que ce séjour soit parfait. Je voudrais voyager en avion ; il me faut absolument un billet en première classe pour voyager de Paris à New York.

Quand je serai aux Etats-Unis, je voudrais loger dans un hôtel cinq étoiles et je voudrais qu'il soit près des magasins. Je voudrais faire du shopping à New York ! Pas plus de cinq minutes à pied maximum.

C'est la première fois que je vais à New York donc je suis, bien sûr, très enthousiaste à l'idée de partir visiter la grosse pomme. J'ai hâte de voir les bâtiments célèbres tels que l'Empire State Building et la statue de la Liberté. J'ai toujours rêvé de me promener ou de faire du patin à glace à Central Park. Par ailleurs, les musées des beaux-arts comptent parmi les meilleurs musées du monde. J'ai envie d'aller y admirer des œuvres d'art moderne.

Enfin, quand je serai à New York, je voudrais goûter la cuisine américaine et manger dans des restaurants connus où se retrouvent des gens célèbres.

Je suis sur un petit nuage, quand je pense que je vais aller aux Etats-Unis. J'adore voyager pour parler la langue du pays et pour rencontrer des gens, New York me paraît une ville pleine d'énergie, donc je compte y passer un super bon séjour !

# Your best holiday

This section will focus on past holidays and the places you have most enjoyed visiting. We'll also look again at the past tenses: the perfect and the imperfect.

| | |
|---|---|
| Mes vacances préférées, c'était ... | My favourite holiday was ... |
| quand je suis allé(e) ... | when I went ... |
| en Grèce | to Greece |
| à Majorque | to Majorca |
| en Crète | to Crete |
| en voyage scolaire | on a school trip |
| C'était ... | It was ... |
| amusant | fun |
| merveilleux | wonderful |
| Il faisait (très chaud) | The weather was (very hot) |
| Il y avait du soleil | The weather was sunny |
| froid | cold |
| J'ai logé dans un hôtel | I stayed in a hotel |
| dans un appartement en location | a self-catering apartment |
| J'ai visité (le château) | I visited (the castle) |
| J'ai nagé dans la mer | I swam in the sea |
| J'ai bronzé/je suis allé(e) bronzer à la piscine | I sunbathed by the pool |
| Je préfère les vacances mouvementées | I prefer active holidays |
| ... les vacances reposantes | ... relaxing holidays |
| ... les vacances à l'étranger | ... holidays abroad |
| ... les vacances en Ecosse | ... holidays in Scotland |

**Grammar blast!**

## The perfect tense and the imperfect tense

This table gives you some of the rules, in this context, as to when you use the perfect tense (passé composé) or the imperfect tense (imparfait).

| Tense | Use it to describe ... | Example | English |
|---|---|---|---|
| **Perfect tense** | Something which happened once | Je suis allé à Paris. | I went to Paris. |
| | Something which happened a specific number of times | Je suis allé à Paris trois fois. | I went to Paris three times. |
| | Something which happened at a specific time | Je suis allé à Paris le lundi. | I went to Paris on Monday. |
| **Imperfect tense** | Something which happened regularly | J'allais à Paris chaque année. | I went to Paris every year. |
| | Something which has no specific ending | J'allais à Paris. | I was going to Paris. |
| | Descriptions | C'était un séjour intéressant. | It was an interesting trip. |
| | Describing the weather | Il faisait beau. | The weather was nice. |

Work out which tense you should use in each of the sentences below: imperfect or perfect?

1. *L'année dernière, j'allais/je suis allé(e) en France dans le cadre d'un échange scolaire.*
2. *J'ai mangé/Je mangeais au restaurant tous les soirs.*
3. *La cuisine était/a été délicieuse !*
4. *Il a fait/Il faisait assez chaud.*
5. *J'ai rendu visite/Je rendais visite à mon grand-père le week-end.*

Gordon, a Scottish student is talking about a trip he took last year to Spain with his friends. Pick out all the phrases in the perfect and imperfect tense and then check your answers online.

*Je suis allé en vacances récemment avec mes amis et mes camarades de classe. Nous sommes allés à Barcelone en Espagne ! L'Espagne se trouve sur la côte méditerranéenne, alors il y faisait très chaud. J'y ai beaucoup aimé les gens, les sites touristiques et la culture.*

*J'ai logé dans un appartement en location avec mes amis et j'ai partagé une chambre avec mon ami, Michael. Malheureusment, il ronflait en dormant et je n'arrivais pas à dormir ! C'était agaçant !*

*Pendant la journée, nous avons fait des activités culturelles et touristiques. Le soir, je suis allé voir un concert que donnait mon DJ préféré, DJ Donna Dongé. J'ai dansé pendant des heures ! C'était un séjour fantastique et j'ai très envie de retourner en Espagne un de ces jours.*

Choose your dream holiday destination and then use the vocabulary from this section to write a short description of where you went, where you stayed, who you went with, what the weather was like, what you did when you were there and what kind of holidays you prefer.

**TOP TIP**

When talking about holidays, you will refer to most of the activities in the perfect tense. All descriptions, things you did repeatedly (e.g. swam in the pool every day) and the weather will be in the imperfect tense.

# Aspects of other countries

The aspects of other countries topic looks at France and other francophone countries. Let's firstly look at France. To do this, we're going to link it to numbers and dates.

Read through the information below about France and then complete the table.

## La France

**Nom :** *République française*

**Devise :** *'Liberté, égalité, fraternité'*

**Drapeau :** *Bleu, blanc et rouge, rayé dans cet ordre verticalement*

**Population :** *65 millions*

**Capitale :** *Paris, où habitent 2 millions de personnes.*

**Gouvernement :** *Démocratie*

**Langue(s) officielle(s) :** *Le français (depuis 1536)*

**Monnaie :** *L'euro (depuis 2002)*

**Organisation :** *Il y a vingt-sept régions en France, notamment l'Ile de France (Paris et ses environs), la Bretagne, la Basse-Normandie et la Haute-Normandie et Rhône-Alpes.*

*5 de ces régions ne sont pas en France mais se trouvent à l'étranger. On appelle ces régions 'outre-mer'. Les régions (et départements) d'outre-mer sont la Guyane française, la Martinique, la Guadeloupe, la Réunion et Mayotte.*

*Chaque région est composée de plusieurs départements. Il y a 101 départements au total.*

| Number | What does it refer to? |
|---|---|
| 65 millions | |
| 2 millions | |
| 1536 | |
| 2002 | |
| 5 | |
| 101 | |

**Grammar blast!**

## Large numbers

When you are writing large numbers, the following rules apply:
- *cent* – takes an s when plural, e.g. *deux cents*
- *mille* – remains unchanged when plural, e.g. *trois mille*
- *millions* – takes an s when plural, e.g. *cinq millions*

*Mais, faites attention!* When cent is followed by another number, it loses the 's', e.g. *deux cent deux* = 202.

**TOP TIP**

An easy way to remember the large numbers rules about whether they take an 's' or not is to think, 'hundreds, a thousand, millions'.

Listen to the following statistics about food in French culture and add in the missing numbers.

1.  *Il y a environ _____ boulangeries en France et on estime que _____ des Français mangent du pain tous les jours !*
2.  *Il y a plus de _____ restaurants à Paris.*
3.  *Les Français mangent l'équivalent de _____ de fromage par personne et par an.*
4.  *Il y a plus de _____ sortes de fromages différents en France.*

**Grammar blast!**

**Years**

Years are said in full in French, e.g.:
*   *deux mille quinze* = 2015
*   *mille neuf cent vingt* = 1920

Look at the following years. Write them out and then practise saying them.

2014

1932

2000

1965

1999

Now listen to the French historian, *le professeur Relique-Ancienne*, talking about important dates from the history of France and add the missing dates and years.

*Les grands événements de l'histoire de France ? Oh, voyons, il y en a beaucoup !*

*La Révolution française a commencé en ____1____ et s'est terminée en ____2____.*

*Le roi de France, Louis XVI et sa femme, Marie-Antoinette, ont été exécutés pendant la Révolution. Louis XVI d'abord, le ____3____ et puis Marie-Antoinette, neuf mois plus tard, le ____4____.*

*Les guerres napoléoniennes sont une série de batailles et guerres qui ont eu lieu entre la France et la Grande-Bretagne entre ____5____ et ____6____. La dernière bataille est celle de Waterloo qui a eu lieu le ____7____ à Waterloo en Belgique.*

*Le Première Guerre mondiale, entre ____8____ et ____9____ puis la Seconde Guerre mondiale entre ____10____ et ____11____ ont été toutes les deux très difficiles pour la France parce qu'une grande partie des combats se sont déroulés en France.*

# La francophonie

'La francophonie' refers to all other countries in the world where French is an official language or French is spoken by a significant number of the population. 57 countries in the world are members of the *Organisation internationale de la francophonie*.

| Les pays francophones … | French-speaking countries … |
|---|---|
| du monde | in the world |
| en Afrique | in Africa |
| en Asie | in Asia |
| en Amérique du Nord | in North America |
| en Amérique du Sud | in South America |
| en Europe | in Europe |
| le français est la deuxième langue européenne | French is the second European language |

## Exercise 1

Look at the list of francophone countries below. Do you know where they are in the world? Write a sentence for each of them, saying which continent they are in.

*E.g. La Belgique **se trouve** en Europe.*

| | |
|---|---|
| la Belgique | le Laos |
| la Suisse | la Canada |
| la Tunisie | le Vietnam |
| la Grèce | le Maroc |
| la Bulgarie | le Luxembourg |
| la Roumanie | Madagascar |
| la Côte d'Ivoire | le Cambodge |

**TOP TIP**

Remember that for feminine countries and continents you use 'en', for masculine countries you use 'au' and for plural countries you use 'aux'.

## Exercise 2

Now read the following accounts of three different francophone countries from around the world and answer the questions below by selecting the correct country for each one.

1.  Which country has the largest population?
2.  Which country has the smallest capital city?
3.  Which country has a lot of poverty?
4.  Which country has the largest number of official languages?
5.  Which country has a royal family?
6.  Which country is mountainous?

### Amira, le Maroc

Le Maroc se trouve en Afrique du Nord. C'est un pays de 33 millions d'habitants. La capitale s'appelle Rabat et se trouve dans l'ouest du pays, sur la côte atlantique. Au Maroc, les langues officielles sont l'arabe et le berbère mais le français est largement parlé aussi. Au Maroc, nous avons une famille royale et un gouvernement. Au Maroc, vous trouverez tout ! Les plages, le désert et, bien sûr, les belles montagnes de l'Atlas !

### Roger, la République démocratique du Congo

Moi, j'habite une grande ville qui s'appelle Kinshasa et qui est la capitale de mon pays, la République démocratique du Congo. Kinshasa est une très grande ville de 8 millions d'habitants. La population du Congo est de 65 millions au total. J'aime habiter ici parce que les gens sont toujours de bonne humeur et qu'il y règne un esprit de communauté, mais c'est vrai qu'il y a beaucoup de pauvreté. Le Congo est un pays d'Afrique, situé dans le sud-ouest du continent. C'est un pays énorme et une grande partie est recouverte par la jungle ! Il n'y a qu'une langue officielle au Congo : le français !

### Olivier, la Suisse

La Suisse est un pays assez petit de 8 millions d'habitants. La Suisse se trouve en plein cœur de l'Europe et c'est un pays alpin et montagneux ! Moi, j'habite dans une ville qui s'appelle Montreux et qui est située au bord d'un lac. La capitale de la Suisse s'appelle Berne, qui ne compte que 125,000 habitants. C'est très petit comme capitale ! Il y a quatre langues officielles en Suisse : le français, l'allemand, l'italien et une langue qui s'appelle le romanche qui est parlée dans certains régions.

# Celebrating special events

'*Jours fériés*' are an important part of all cultures. Let's have a look at the main French festivals.

| | |
|---|---|
| *un jour férié* | a public holiday |
| *une fête* | a party/festival |
| *fêter* | to celebrate |
| *un jour de congé* | a day off |
| *le réveillon* | Christmas Eve party |
| *le Nouvel An* | New Year |
| *les traditions* | traditions |
| *faire la fête* | have a party |
| *On s'amuse bien !* | We enjoy ourselves! |

## Exercise 1

| La date | La fête |
|---|---|
| *Le 1er janvier* | *Le Jour de l'An.* |
| *Le 6 janvier* | *L'Epiphanie* |
| *février* | *la Chandeleur* |
| | *La Saint-Valentin* |
| *avril* | *Le 1er avril – Poisson d'avril* |
| *le 1er mai* | *La Fête du Travail* |
| *le 8 mai* | *L'Armistice* |
| *juin* | *La Fête de la musique* |
| *juillet le 14 juilliet* | *La fête nationale* |
| *novembre* | *La Toussaint* |
| *novembre* | *Le 11 Novembre* |
| *le 24 décembre* | *La veille de Noël* |
| *le 25 décembre* | *Le jour de Noël* |
| *le 31 janvier* | *Le réveillon du Nouvel An* |

Look at the French calendar of festivals above. Read about the traditions below and match them to each of the festivals to complete the calendar.

1. *La soirée précédant Noël quand on se retrouve en famille pour dîner et pour échanger des cadeaux.*
2. *Jour qui commémore la Révolution et l'établissement de la république française. Il y a des feux d'artifice.*
3. *Une journée en famille pour manger et fêter Noël !*
4. *On fête le premier jour de l'année !*
5. *Fête qui marque la fin des fêtes de Noël et l'arrivée des rois mages.*
6. *Un jour de congé qui veut dire en fait qu'il n'y a pas de travail pour la plupart des gens aujourd'hui !*
7. *Fête romantique quand on achète des cadeaux et des fleurs pour nos amoureux(euses).*
8. *Jour commémorant la fin de la Première Guerre mondiale. Le président de la République dépose une gerbe de fleurs sur la tombe du Soldat inconnu à l'Arc de triomphe à Paris.*
9. *Journée où l'on mange des crêpes.*
10. *Un jour férié où l'on se souvient des amis ou des membres de sa famille décédés.*
11. *Un jour férié commémorant la fin de la Seconde Guerre mondiale en Europe.*
12. *Une nuit festive qui arrive à son point culminant à minuit avec l'arrivée du Nouvel An !*

13. *Faites attention ! C'est la journée des blagues et des tours !*
14. *Fête où l'on organise des concerts dans toutes les villes françaises. Une nuit pour danser et écouter de la musique !*

**Grammar blast!**

### Reflexive verbs in the perfect tense

'*s'amuser*' is an example of a reflexive verb in French. Let's now look at how reflexive verbs are formed in the perfect tense. You'll notice that they all take '*être*' in the perfect tense.

As the reflexive verbs take '*être*', this also means they have to agree with their subject. The agreements are in brackets in the example of *s'amuser* below.

| s'amuser | | | |
|---|---|---|---|
| *Je me suis amusé(e)* | I enjoyed myself | *Nous nous sommes amusé(e)(s)* | We enjoyed ourselves |
| *Tu t'es amusé(e)* | You enjoyed yourself | *Vous vous êtes amusé(e)(s)* | You enjoyed yourself/ yourselves |
| *Il/Elle s'est amusé(e)* | He/she enjoyed him/ herself | *Ils/Elles se sont amusé(e)(s)* | They enjoyed themselves |
| *On s'est amusé* | One enjoyed oneself We enjoyed ourselves | | |

### Exercise 2

Fill in the correct form of '*s'amuser*' in the perfect tense in the sentences below.

1. *Je _____ à la Fête de la musique !*
2. *Nous _____ le jour de la Saint-Valentin cette année !*
3. *Est-ce que tu _____ au réveillon ?*
4. *Je sais que Thomas _____ à l'Epiphanie !*
5. *Elles _____ en faisant des crêpes pour la Chandeleur !*

**TOP TIP**

You will know a verb is reflexive when you look it up in the dictionary because it will have the pronoun 'se' before the infinitive, e.g. se coucher or s'amuser.

# Literature of France

The 'literature of France' topic gives you a chance to delve a bit deeper into the history and traditions of French literature and culture.

| | |
|---|---|
| *un roman* | a novel |
| *un livre non romanesque* | a non-fiction book |
| *écrit par* | written by |
| *l'histoire* | the story |
| *l'intrigue* | the plot |
| *une comédie* | a comedy |
| *un roman d'aventures* | an adventure novel |
| *un livre pour enfants* | a children's book |
| *un roman policier* | a murder mystery |
| *une histoire qui fait peur* | a scary story |
| *une histoire d'amour* | a love story |
| *le roman a lieu en France* | the novel is set in France |
| *l'action se déroule à Paris* | the action takes place in Paris |
| *les descriptions sont très (vivantes)* | the descriptions are very (vivid) |
| *c'est une histoire (captivante)* | it's a (gripping) story |
| *compliqué(e)* | complicated |
| *amusant(e)* | funny |
| *l'histoire me tient en haleine* | the story grips me |
| *mon auteur préféré c'est* | my favourite author is |
| *mon livre préféré c'est* | my favourite book is |

## Exercise 1

Make a list of five books you've read, and use the vocabulary on the previous page to write a sentence about each one.

## Exercise 2

Read the following opinions about books. Think of a book you have read that matches this opinion and write the title in the Livre column.

| Opinion | Livre |
|---|---|
| A mon avis, c'est une histoire assez longue et trop compliquée. | |
| Selon moi, c'est un roman avec une intrigue passionnante et vous tient en haleine. | |
| D'après moi, l'histoire est romantique mais un peu niaise. | |
| Je trouve les personnages très amusants. | |
| Je m'identifie au personnage principal. | |

## Exercise 3

The following books are classic French novels. Use a dictionary to translate the titles into English and then look them up online to see if you can find out what kind of book they are (e.g. *science fiction, roman historique, roman d'amour*) and who wrote them.

### TOP TIP

Reading a French book or story that you have already read in an English translation is a good way of helping you to improve your reading skills.

| Titre | Traduction | Auteur | Genre |
|---|---|---|---|
| 1. Le Tour du monde en quatre-vingts jours | | | |
| 2. Les Trois Mousquetaires | | | |
| 3. Le Comte de Monte-Cristo | | | |
| 4. Vingt mille lieues sous les mers | | | |
| 5. Le Petit Nicolas | | | |
| 6. Le Petit prince | | | |

## Exercise 4

Now listen to this French teenager, Mathieu, talking about his favourite French book and answer the questions below in English.

1. How often does Mathieu try to read a book? (1)
2. What types of books does he like? (2)
3. What did *80 Days Around the World* inspire him to do? (1)
4. What other kinds of books does he enjoy? (2)
5. What does he like about *The 3 Musketeers* and *The Man in the Iron Mask*? (2)
6. Why does he prefer *Le Petit Nicolas*? (2)

## Exercise 5

Read about French teenager Pierre talking about French literature and then answer the questions.

*Je crois que mon auteur français préféré c'est un auteur, très connu, en France, qui s'appelle Daniel Pennac. Son style est très facile à lire et je trouve que les intrigues sont toujours très bien construites. J'adore son roman 'L'Œil du loup'. C'est l'histoire de l'amitié entre un enfant africain et un loup qu'il rencontre quand il va au zoo. Pour moi, l'idée du roman est vraiment originale et dès que j'ai commencé à le lire, je n'ai pas pu m'arrêter.*

1. Who is Pierre's favourite author? Give details. (1)
2. What does he think of his writing style and storylines? (2)
3. What is his book *'L'Œil du loup'* about? (2)
4. What else does he say about the book? (2)
5. Which of the following questions do you think Pierre was responding to? Tick the correct box. (1)

> 1. What kind of books do you enjoy reading? ☐
> 2. What do you think of French books for young people? ☐
> 3. Tell us about your favourite French author. ☐

# Film

The final topic looks at French film and TV. First, we look at Film. In class you may have watched French films and clips from TV programmes.

| | |
|---|---|
| *Mon film français préféré c'est* | My favourite French film is |
| *un film d'épouvante/d'horreur* | a horror film |
| *une comédie* | a comedy |
| *une comédie romantique* | a romantic comedy |
| *un drame* | a drama |
| *un film d'action* | an action film |
| *un film d'amour* | a love film |
| *un film de science-fiction* | science fiction |
| *un film policier* | a police film |
| *un dessin-animé* | a cartoon |
| *les personnages* | the characters |
| *le scénario* | film script |
| *la mise-en-scène* | the production |
| *un acteur/une actrice* | an actor/an actress |
| *la vedette* | the star |
| *le réalisateur/la réalisatrice* | the director |
| *les sous-titres* | subtitles |
| *le film se passe (en France)* | the film is set (in France) |
| *le film m'a fait (rire/pleurer/peur)* | the film made me (laugh/cry/scared) |
| *Je préfère voir les films au cinéma* | I prefer watching films at the cinema |
| *J'ai vu un film au cinéma* | I saw a film at the cinema |

## Exercise 1

Do an Internet search for the following French films and complete the table below with the missing information.

| Titre du film | Réalisateur | Genre | Tu l'as vu ? |
|---|---|---|---|
| Une vie de chat | | | Je l'ai vu /Je ne l'ai pas vu |
| Le Petit Nicolas | | | |
| Au revoir les enfants | | | |
| Les Choristes | | | |

## Exercise 2

Now write a mimumum of four sentences in French about a French film you have seen. Use the example below to help you.

1. J'ai vu un film français qui s'appelle Les Choristes.
2. Le film se passe en France pendant les années cinquante.
3. Le film a été réalisé par Christophe Barratier et la vedette du film, c'est l'acteur français Gérard Jugnot.
4. C'est un drame mais c'est aussi très amusant par moments.

**Grammar blast!**

### The imperfect tense

The imperfect tense is used for descriptions and opinions in the past. For regular verbs, it is formed by taking the 'nous' part of the verb in the present tense and then adding the endings below. Let's take the example of 'regarder' and look at how it's formed.

1. regarder – nous regardons
2. Take away the 'ons' ending and you're left with the stem 'regard'
3. Then add the following endings:

| regarder (to watch) | | | |
|---|---|---|---|
| je regardais | I watched | nous regardions | we watched |
| tu regardais | you watched | vous regardiez | you watched |
| il/elle regardait | he/she watched | ils/elles regardaient | they watched |
| on regardait | one/we watched | | |

être is the only irregular verb in the imperfect tense. The stem is ét and you just add the same endings as above, e.g. J'étais, tu étais, il était, etc.

**TOP TIP**

Remember, if the subject of a sentence is a singular noun (e.g. le film) then it takes the il or elle part of the verb, e.g. Le film était très drôle.

## Exercise 3

Complete the following sentences by adding the imperfect tense of the verb in brackets. Conjugate the verb in full first if it helps you.

1. L'action _____ (se dérouler) pendant la Révolution française.
2. A mon avis, le film _____ (être) bien construit.
3. Les enfants _____ (chanter) dans une chorale.
4. Il y _____ (avoir) une scène très émouvante à la fin du film.
5. Le personnage principal _____ (retrouver) sa famille.

## Exercise 4

Read the following opinions of films and translate them into English. Write the name of a film that reflects this opinion for you.

| Opinion (French) | Opinion (English) | Film |
|---|---|---|
| 1. J'ai trouvé ce film trop long et l'histoire était difficile à suivre. | | |
| 2. J'avais du mal à lire les sous-titres. | | |
| 3. J'aimais le personnage principal et je m'indentifiais à son dilemme. | | |
| 4. L'intrigue était très bien écrite avec beaucoup de rebondissements ! | | |
| 5. J'étais déçu par la fin du film. | | |
| 6. Je me sentais un peu bouleversé(e) par ce film. | | |
| 7. Je rigolais sans arrêt en regardant ce film ! | | |

# Television

Finally, let's look at television in France.

| | |
|---|---|
| J'aime regarder … | I like to watch … |
| … les émissions | … programmes |
| … les émissions de sport | … sports programmes |
| … les émissions sur les voitures | … car programmes |
| … les émissions sur la nature | … nature programmes |
| … les informations | … the news |
| … les débats politiques | … political debates |
| … les séries policières | … American series |
| … les émissions policères | … detective shows |
| … la télé-réalité | … reality TV |
| … les dessins animés | … cartoons |
| … les jeux télévisé | … gameshows/quiz shows |
| … les comédies | … comedies |
| … les documentaires | … documentaries |
| … les feuilletons | … soap operas |
| … les sitcoms | … sitcoms |
| … les thrillers psychologiques | … thrillers |
| … les publicités | … the adverts |
| … les présentateurs | … the presenters |
| Cela plaît beaucoup aux jeunes | It's very popular with young people |
| Ça a l'air (divertissant) | It looks (entertaining) |
| Ça me paraît être (bête) | It seems to me to be (stupid) |
| Je ne regarderais jamais cette émission | I would never watch this programme |
| J'aimerais bien la voir | I would really like to see it |
| zapper | to flick through the channels |

Look up the following French TV shows on the Internet. Write what type of programme it is and give your opinion on whether you would like to watch it or not.

| Emission | Genre | Opinion? |
|---|---|---|
| E.g. *Les Revenants* | *thriller psychologique* | *J'aime ce type d'émission.* |
| *the Voice* | | |
| *Plus belle la vie* | | |
| *Des chiffres et des lettres* | | |
| *Qui veut gagner des millions ?* | | |
| *Dora l'exploratrice* | | |
| *La Planète bleue* | | |
| *Téléfoot* | | |
| *Le journal de 13 heures* | | |
| *Danse avec les stars* | | |

Now listen to the following people giving their opinions about TV programmes. Listen and then complete the table.

| Type(s) of programme | Opinion (When they watch TV/ how often/where) | Opinion of TV |
|---|---|---|
| 1. **Jean**<br>2. **Béa**<br>3. **Paul** | | |

### Exercise 3

Decide if each of the following opinons about TV are negative or positive and then give an example of any programme which matches that opinion for you.

|  | Negative | Positive | Example |
|---|---|---|---|
| C'est une émission bête que je ne regarderais jamais. |  |  |  |
| Je ne rate jamais cette émission. |  |  |  |
| Je ne l'ai pas vue mais j'ai envie de la voir. |  |  |  |
| Je regarde cette émission quand je zappe et que je ne trouve rien de plus intéressant à regarder. |  |  |  |

## TOP TIP

French channels like TF1 and Canal+ have lots of programmes which you can watch via their websites. Watching French TV online is a really good way to help expose you to the language and gradually build up your understanding and familiarity with French. Pick a programme you like in English and watch its French equivalent – French football programmes, such as *Téléfoot*, or a feuilleton like *Plus Belle la Vie*.

### Exercise 4

Now read the following article about television and answer the questions in English.

*Les jeunes ados regardent la télévision plus que jamais auparavant. 'Je regarde des DVD de séries américaines. Je les regarde sur mon ordinateur portable, au lit, dans ma chambre.' dit Anaïs, une lycéenne de Reims. 'Le problème c'est que maintenant, je ne pense plus à rien quand je reste au lit en regardant des séries pendant deux, trois, quatre heures. Quand je commence, je n'arrive pas à m'arrêter ! C'est addictif !' Cette situation devient de plus en plus courante chez les jeunes, qui regardent la télé en moyenne trente-quatre heures et demie par semaine. 'Un peu de télé peut permettre de se détendre et ça peut être éducatif mais c'est comme tout : il faut de la modération,' conseille un expert.*

1. What type of TV does Anaïs watch? Where does she watch it? (2)
2. What does she say is the problem with this? (2)
3. What does the report say about how much time teenagers spend watching TV? (1)
4. What points does the expert make about TV? Mention any 2 things. (2)
5. What is the main purpose of this report? Tick the correct box. (1)

> 1. To warn about the kind of programmes young people are watching. ■
> 2. To warn about the TV viewing habits of young people. ■
> 3. To look at the different ways young people are watching TV. ■

# Focus on grammar: the perfect tense and the imperfect tense

The final focus on grammar will look more in depth at the two main past tenses in French – the perfect tense and the imperfect tense.

It can be tricky to distinguish between which tense to use and when, but these English translations should help guide you.

| Tense | Perfect | Imperfect |
|---|---|---|
| Example | J'ai travaillé | Je travaillais |
| Translation | I was working | I have worked<br>I worked<br>I did work |

Now let's look at each of them in more detail.

## The perfect tense

The table below outlines when we would use the perfect tense (*passé* compose).

**TOP TIP**

Learning grammar can seem like a huge task but, like everything in language learning, the more you see it and use it, the more it becomes part of your active vocabulary.

| | | |
|---|---|---|
| Something that happened once. | Je suis allé à Paris. | I went to Paris. |
| Something that happened a specific number of times. | Je suis allé à Paris trois fois. | I went to Paris three times. |
| Something that happened at a specific time. | Je suis allé à Paris lundi. | I went to Paris on Monday. |

### Exercise 1

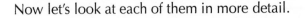

Read the following sentences and decide if they would be in the perfect tense or not, if translated. Explain why for each of them, and then add a translation.

| Sentence | Perfect tense? | Explanation | Translation |
|---|---|---|---|
| Last night I went to the cinema to watch the French film, *Tais toi !* | | | |
| I ate at the restaurant one or two times. | | | |
| We went during the summer. | | | |
| My friends visited their cousins. | | | |
| I was living in Paris. | | | |

# Perfect tense with avoir

The perfect tense with *avoir* is the most common form of the perfect tense and applies to all French verbs except the group of *être* verbs (more on this later) and reflexive verbs (e.g. *se lever*).

To conjugate the perfect tense, you first of all need to know *avoir* and secondly need to know the past participle of the verb.

To form the past participle of a regular ER, RE and IR verbs, apply the following rules:

| Regular verb | Rule | Past participle |
|---|---|---|
| ER verbs, e.g. *manger* | ER becomes *é* | *mangé* |
| RE verbs, e.g. *rendre* | RE becomes *u* | *rendu* |
| IR verbs, e.g. *finir* | IR becomes *i* | *fini* |

## Exercise 2

Organise the following verbs into the correct columns of the table below and then add an example of what one would look like in the full version of the perfect tense. Finally, translate your example.

| | | | | | |
|---|---|---|---|---|---|
| *manger* | *parler* | *perdre* | *répondre* | *réfléchir* | *visiter* |
| *rendre* | *voyager* | *fêter* | *finir* | *entendre* | *établir* |
| *choisir* | *vendre* | *attendre* | *regarder* | *grossir* | *maigrir* |

| *Avoir* | ER verbs | RE verbs | IR verbs | Example | Translation |
|---|---|---|---|---|---|
| *j'ai* | *mangé* | *rendu* | *maigri* | *J'ai maigri* | I lost weight |
| *tu as* | | | | | |
| *il/elle/on a* | | | | | |
| *nous avons* | | | | | |
| *vous avez* | | | | | |
| *ils/elles ont* | | | | | |

## Exercise 3

Using the table above and the bank of time phrases (right) to help you, translate the following sentences.

1. We travelled last week.
2. I lost weight during the holidays.
3. They (f) celebrated at the weekend.
4. He answered three days ago.
5. She visited the castle two weeks ago.
6. You ate a pizza yesterday.
7. She sold the house in the morning.
8. They (m) chose the book a month ago.

> **Time phrases**
> *il y a un mois* – one month ago
> *la semaine dernière* – last week
> *il y a deux semaines* – two weeks ago
> *pendant les vacances* – during the holidays
> *le week-end* – at the weekend
> *le matin* – in the morning
> *hier* – yesterday
> *il y a trois jours* – three days ago

# Irregular past participles with avoir

The following verbs have irregular past participles and so don't follow the rules opposite.
Complete the table below with an example of each and the translation.

| Infinitive | Past participle | Example | Translation |
|---|---|---|---|
| avoir | eu | j'ai eu | I had |
| boire | bu | | |
| comprendre | compris | | |
| connaître | connu | | |
| croire | cru | | |
| devoir | dû | | |
| dire | dit | | |
| écrire | écrit | | |
| être | été | | |
| faire | fait | | |
| lire | lu | | |
| mettre | mis | | |
| ouvrir | ouvert | | |
| pouvoir | pu | | |
| prendre | pris | | |
| savoir | su | | |
| voir | vu | | |
| vouloir | voulu | | |

# The perfect tense with être

To be or not to be?

Let's now focus on the perfect tense with *être*.

The three key things you need to know about the perfect tense
with *être* are:

1.  Which verbs take *être* in the perfect tense
2.  What their past participles are (e.g. *aller* becomes *allé*)
3.  That they must agree with the subject, i.e. take an 'e' when
    feminine and an 's' when plural (e.g. *elle est allée*)
4.  Let's start with the verbs that take *être* in the perfect tense.

Complete the parts of être in the table below:

| *être* | To be | | |
|---|---|---|---|
| | I am<br>you are<br>he/she is<br>one is/we are | | we are<br>you are<br>they are |

Below, you'll find a group of the main verbs which take être in the perfect tense. There is no easy way around this, other than just to learn these verbs! It's painful but the best approach is to choose a way that works for you and practise, practise, practise until you've got them. The verbs below are arranged so that their first letters each spell out MRS VANDERTRAMP. Some people find this a useful way to learn them!

| Verb | Past participle | Example |
|---|---|---|
| **M**onter | monté | je suis monté**(e)** |
| **R**etourner | retourné | tu es retourné**(e)** |
| **S**ortir | sorti | il est sorti |
| **V**enir | venu | elle est venu**e** |
| **A**rriver | arrivé | on est arrivé |
| **N**aître | né | nous sommes né**(e)s** |
| **D**escendre | descendu | vous êtes descendu**(e)s** |
| **E**ntrer | entré | ils sont entré**s** |
| **R**ester | resté | elles sont resté**es** |
| **T**omber | tombé | je suis tombé**(e)** |
| **R**entrer | rentré | tu es rentré**(e)** |
| **A**ller | allé | il est allé |
| **M**ourir | mort | elle est morte |
| **P**artir | parti | on est parti |

## Exercise 6

Take all of the examples from the table above and rewrite them using a different pronoun and part of être. Don't forget that they have to agree with the subject.

For example:

| Our example | Your example |
|---|---|
| Je suis monté**(e)** | Elle est montée |

## Exercise 7

Write out a list of all the verbs that take être from the table above and try each of the following approaches to learn them. There are 14 verbs so give each approach a rating out of 14 e.g. Cinq sur quatorze, based on how many you remembered.

**Approach**

Write the verbs into two lists of opposites, e.g. mourir/naître, arriver/partir. Add an action to each of them and try and learn all seven pairs with their accompanying actions. Note: tomber and rester don't really match with anything so put them together.

Draw a house with stick people showing each of the actions from the verbs, e.g. monter/descendre can be shown on stairs.

Using the verbs with Je (as in the rhyme below), write a short story going through all the actions and just the verbs, e.g. going into a house, going up the stairs would be je suis entré, je suis monté, etc.

**Approach**

Try adding a rhythm to the verbs as they are grouped below or creating your own actions or tune to go along with them.

*je suis allé*
*je suis venu*
*je suis monté*
*je suis descendu*

*je suis entré*
*je suis sorti*
*je suis arrivé*
*je suis parti*

*je suis tombé*
*je suis resté*
*je suis rentré*
*je suis retourné*

*je suis né*
*je suis mort*

---

### Exercise 8

Read the following text by a Scottish teenage girl, Sophie. It's full of mistakes! Find the 10 mistakes in the perfect tense with être and rewrite the text in the correct form.

*Pendant les grandes vacances, je suis alles en France avec ma famille. C'était vraiment super ! Nous sont arrivé le lundi et nous avons monté à la Tour Eiffel le jour même ! Quand je suis descendus de la tour, j'ai tombé et j'ai cassé mon appareil photo malheureusement. Ma famille et moi sont resté à Paris pendant une semaine mais ma soeur a partie la semaine suivante. Elle a retourné en Ecosse en train et nous sommes rentré en avion. Quand je suis quitter Paris, j'étais triste. J'y retournerai un de ces jours !*

**TOP TIP**

When you want to make anything in the perfect tense negative, simply add 'ne' and 'pas' around the auxilary verb (the être or avoir part) e.g. Je *n'ai pas* voyagé, je *ne* suis pas allé !

# The imperfect tense

Finally, let's focus on the imperfect tense. It's fairly straightforward once you've learnt a few simple rules.

The imperfect tense is used in the following cases:

1. To describe something that happened regularly in the past, e.g. *je jouais avec mes amis tous les jours* (I used to play with my friends everyday)
2. To describe what something was like in the past, e.g. *C'était formidable mais il faisait très chaud !* (It was great but the weather was very hot !)
3. To describe things with no definite end, e.g. *J'étais en France* (I was in France)

Exercise 9

Write five sentences in English that would be translations of the imperfect tense in French. Explain why each of them is imperfect.

| Sentence | Explanation |
|---|---|
| E.g. I was in France. | No definite end so would be classed as ongoing/incomplete. |

## Forming the imperfect tense

To form the imperfect tense, follow these steps:

1. Find the *nous* form of the verb in the present tense, e.g. *nous travaillons*.
2. Chop off the **ons** ending.
3. Add the following endings:

| Infinitive | *parler* | *attendre* | *finir* |
|---|---|---|---|
| **Present nous form** | *parl**ons*** | *attend**ons*** | *finiss**ons*** |
| **Imperfect** | *je parl**ais*** | *j'attend**ais*** | *je finiss**ais*** |
| | *tu parl**ais*** | *tu attend**ais*** | *tu finiss**ais*** |
| | *il/elle/on parl**ait*** | *il/elle/on attend**ait*** | *il/elle/on finiss**ais*** |
| | *nous parl**ions*** | *nous attend**ions*** | *nous finiss**ions*** |
| | *vous parl**iez*** | *vous attend**iez*** | *vous finiss**iez*** |
| | *ils/elles parl**aient*** | *ils/elles attend**aient*** | *ils/elles finiss**aient*** |

## TOP TIP

- ER verbs which have the letter G before the ER, keep the E part in the *nous* form, e.g. *Nous mangeons* in the imperfect would be *'je mangeais'*.
- Remember that *être* is the only irregular verb in the imperfect tense. Its stem is *ét* in the imperfect and so it becomes *'j'étais, tu étais'*, etc.
- *'Il y a'* becomes *'il y avait'* in the imperfect and translates as 'there was/were'. A very useful phrase to know!

### Exercise 10

Pick any five verbs and complete your own version of the table below. The first one has been started for you so you can use it as a guide.

| | |
|---|---|
| **Infinitive** | écouter |
| **Present nous form** | écout**ons** |
| **Imperfect** | j'écout**ais** |

### Exercise 11

Think back to the festivals you celebrated when you were young. Complete the following sentences, adding in the correct forms of the verbs in the imperfect tense.

Quand j'_____(1) jeune, _____(2) beaucoup de fêtes ! Pour le Nouvel An, ma mère _____(3) toujours une soirée pour toute la famille chez nous. Mon beau-père _____(4) des feux d'artifice dans le jardin à minuit ! (5) fantastique ! J'adore manger, alors la Chandeleur _____(6) une de mes fêtes préférées. On_____ (7) des crêpes au chocolat, _____(8) trop bon !

Pour Pâques, nous _____(9) toujours les oeufs et je _____(10) beaucoup d'oeufs au chocolat bien sûr !

La Fête de la musique _____(11) très appréciée dans ma ville et j' _____(12) souvent à des concerts. J'_____(13) écouter la musique et danser avec mes amis au centre-ville !

Enfin, il ne faut pas oublier le plus grand fête, Noël. On _____(14) toujours Noël en famille et après un bon repas, moi et mes frères _____(15) tous nos cadeaux !

| | | | | |
|---|---|---|---|---|
| étais | organisait | allions | passait | ouvrions |
| il y avait | allumait | peignions | était | c'était |
| mangeait | mangeais | aimais | assistais | |

### Exercise 12

Pick any five festivals you celebrated when you were young and write a sentence in the imperfect tense about what you did for each of them.

**TOP TIP**

Keep things simple and use the vocabulary you have to find a way of saying what you want to be able to say. If it feels like it doesn't make sense it probably doesn't, so try a simpler approach!

# Preparing for talking

Your talking assessment is a very important part of your overall modern languages experience. Not only because it is worth a third of your overall mark, but also because it is helping you to develop the skills to become a true French speaker!

## Presentation

Let's look at what you can do to develop your skills in the presentation and to help you ensure you are as well prepared as you can be.

| | |
|---|---|
| Je vais parler de | I'm going to talk about |
| Je voudrais vous parler de | I would like to talk about |
| Je vais vous présenter | I'm going to present to you |
| Je vais discuter de | I'm going to discuss |
| Pour conclure | To conclude |
| En conclusion | In conclusion |

When writing your presentation, use the following success criteria to help you plan and review what you have written:

1. Choose a topic you will enjoy speaking about.
2. Have a clear introduction, at least two structured paragraphs and then a clear conclusion.
3. Use a variety of language structures, e.g. different opinion phrases.
4. Use modifiers, e.g. *très, assez, vraiment* etc.
5. Use interesting adjectives. Don't just stick to sympa, gentil, etc.
6. Use interesting time phrases, e.g. *tous les quinze jours, il y a un an,* etc.
7. Include at least one stand-out phrase that adds a little gold dust!
8. Use at least two tenses, including the conditional, e.g. *J'aimerais.*

### Exercise 1

Read the following sample speaking presentation and check it against the success criteria above. Catagorise the sentences into what works and what can be improved, then rewrite the improvement sentences with your own amendments.

*Je vais discuter de mes passe-temps préférés.*

*D'une manière générale, je dirais que je suis une personne motivée, active et enthousiaste. J'aime passer du temps en plein air et je préfère faire du sport plutôt que de rester clouée devant la télé ou l'ordinateur. Cependant, j'aime beaucoup me détendre et je vais souvent au cinéma.*

*Quant au sport, j'aime faire du vélo, du VTT, de la natation, du footing et je fais aussi partie d'une équipe de foot à cinq. Je suis fan de sports d'hiver comme le ski, mais je n'en fais pas souvent. Je trouve que le sport est non seulement bon pour la santé mais aussi très bon pour l'esprit ! Je suis heureuse quand je fais du sport.*

*En conclusion, j'adore le sport, c'est super !*

**TOP TIP**

- The better prepared you are for your speaking assessment, the less nervous you will be on the day.
- Ask your teacher to listen to you saying your presentation, correct your pronunciation and then record it so you can listen to it at home.
- Breaking it down into small chunks to learn will make it more manageable.
- Avoid sounding monotone and make sure you understand exactly what you are saying.

## Talking: conversation

Your teacher will ask you some unexpected questions. These will often be things like 'who with, when, you like ... ?', etc. Below you will find a list of key words which may come up in these types of questions. Prepare responses to the questions you are most likely to be asked and get a family member or friend to practise them with you.

### Exercise 2

Using the key words below, prepare a bank of answers to these questions, which you can use no matter what the topic is or when they are asked.

**TOP TIP**

Never be afraid to say you don't understand (*Je ne comprends pas*) or to ask your teacher to repeat the question (*Vous pouvez répéter la question, s'il vous plaît?*).

| Key question words | Example | Your response |
|---|---|---|
| *Avec qui ?* | *J'y vais avec mon frère.* | |
| *Quand ?* | *Tous les jours après l'école.* | |
| *Tu aimes (le foot) ?* | *Oui, j'adore ça !* | |
| *Où ?* | *A la maison.* | |

# Preparing for writing

As with the talking assessment, you have time on your side to get ready for the writing. You can prepare most of it in advance!

The writing assessment requires you to answer a job advert by writing an email job application. The job will be different in every question paper but the responses you have to give will largely remain the same.

Firstly, let's look at how you would start your email, depending on what job you are applying for.

| Cher Monsieur/Chère Madame | Sir/Madame |
|---|---|
| *Suite à votre annonce, je me permets de poser ma candidature pour le poste de (réceptionniste).*<br>　*serveur/serveuse*<br>　*vendeur/vendeuse*<br>　*animateur/animatrice* | Following your advert, I would like to apply for the post of (receptionist).<br>　waiter/waitress<br>　shop assistant<br>　group leader |

### Exercise 1

Read the following job adverts and, using the vocabulary above, write the opening line of an email for each one.

# Carrières

**1. Hôtel Coco Chanel**
Cherche de jeunes gens travailleurs et fiables pour travailler dans notre hôtel comme réceptionnistes à partir de la fin du mois de septembre.

**2. Camping Où est ma tente**
Aimez-vous travailler en contact avec des enfants ? Est-ce que vous êtes enthousiaste, avez-vous le sens de l'humour ? Nous recherchons des jeunes pour nous assister en tant qu'animateurs dans notre camping cet été de début juin à fin septembre.

**3. Café L'Escargot rapide**
Nous avons besoin de jeunes qui parlent français et au moins une autre langue pour travailler dans notre charmant petit café. Voici en quoi consiste le travail : servir les clients, préparer les boissons et nettoyer les tables.

**4. Souvenirs de Paris**
Cherche de jeunes gens motivés et travailleurs qui parlent au moins deux langues (le français et l'anglais) pour travailler comme serveur/serveuse dans notre magasin au centre de Paris.

*TOP TIP*
Make sure you use the masculine and feminine job title when you are writing your response, e.g. serveur/serveuse.

# Answering the predictable bullet points

Now let's look in more detail at how you answer each of the bullet points.

Four of the bullet points will always be as follows:

- Personal details (name, age, where you live)
- School/college/education experience until now
- Skills/interests you have which make you right for the job
- Related work experience

The other two will be different each time but will usually relate to work and education.

## Exercise 2

Look at the vocabulary below relating to work experience and skills and match the sentences to the jobs from the adverts on the previous page. You can use them more than once.

**TOP TIP**

You're writing is 120–150 words in total. You can take off 30 words altogether for your introduction and conclusion, meaning you have about 20 words per bullet point to write.

| | |
|---|---|
| *J'ai appris comment parler aux clients* | I learned how to talk to customers |
| *J'ai de l'expérience dans le domaine de l'enfance* | I have experience of working with children |
| *J'ai appris comment utiliser la caisse* | I learned how to use the till |
| *Je travaille bien en équipe* | I work well in a team |
| *Je m'exprime bien* | I express myself well |
| *J'aime parler avec les clients* | I like speaking to customers |
| *Je suis toujours bien habillé(e)* | I'm always well-dressed |

## Exercise 3

Read the following text and match each paragraph to the correct bullet point above. Rewrite the text in the correct order, changing the words in bold to answer it for yourself.

1. *Cette année, j'ai fait un stage **dans un restaurant** et j'y ai appris à **servir les clients** et **l'importance d'être organisé dans son travail**.*
2. *Je suis actuellement élève à **St Anne's High School** où je suis **en troisième**. J'étudie **les maths, l'anglais, le français, l'histoire, la musique et l'allemand**.*
3. *Je suis une personne **motivée, polie et travailleuse** et j'aime **rencontrer des gens**. Je m'intéresse beaucoup **à la mode** ; à mon avis, je suis faite pour travailler **dans un magasin**.*
4. *Je m'appelle **Anna Wenerowski** et j'ai **quinze** ans. J'habite à **Milnathort**, un **petit village situé dans l'est de l'Ecosse**.*

# Answering the unseen/unpredictable bullet points

Let's now focus on the two bullet points that are unseen and unpredictable. These require you to write without knowing what is going to be asked and are a test of your ability to cope with the unknown while still retaining control of the language.

Exercise 4

Read the examples of unseen/unpredictable bullet points below and match each one to the correct translation in the right-hand column.

1. When are you available to start work?
2. Which languages you speak.
3. What experience you have of working with young people.
4. How you get on with customers.
5. What additional tasks you could undertake in the shop.
6. How you would contribute to the day to day running of the hostel.
7. What activities you would play/do with the children.
8. Your experience of other countries.
9. Why you would like to work in France.
10. What links you have with France.

a. *Je rangerais les rayons et je plierais les vêtements.*
b. *J'aime cuisiner et je pourrais préparer le petit-déjeuner le matin.*
c. *Je voudrais travailler en France parce que j'aime découvrir de nouvelles cultures.*
d. *Je suis très sportif, donc je jouerais au ping-pong et au foot avec les enfants.*
e. *Je suis allé en France il y a deux ans et je voudrais visiter les Etats-Unis.*
f. *Je m'entends bien avec les clients car je suis une personne gentille et polie.*
g. *Je peux commencer le travail au mois de juillet, pendant les grandes vacances.*
h. *J'apprends le français depuis 6 ans et j'ai un correspondant à Nice.*
i. *Je parle l'anglais, le français et j'apprends le chinois.*
j. *J'aime le contact avec les enfants et je travaille dans un club pour enfants tous les samedis.*

Exercise 5

Creating a bank like the one started for you below can be a useful way to collect different parts of phrases, which you can then mix and match to possible unseen/unpredictable bullet points. Using the examples of unseen/unpredictable bullet points from exercise 4, see if you can add any more words/phrases to the table below.

| Verbs | Whole verbs | Time phrases | Connectors | Opinions | Places | Adjectives |
|---|---|---|---|---|---|---|
| *Je voudrais* | *commencer* | *le week-end* | *mais* | *A mon avis* | *dans un magasin* | *disponible* |
| *Je travaille* | *travailler* | *au mois de...* | *parce que* | | *dans un café* | *prêt(e)* |
| *Je sers* | | | *cependant* | | | |

## Exercise 6

Use the writing bank created in exercise 5 to see if you can now answer each of the unseen/unpredictable bullet points in exercise 4.

## Exercise 7

Translate the following sentences from English to French.

1. I work in a café at the weekend.
2. I have experience of working with children.
3. I like speaking French.
4. I would like to work in France because I would like to improve my French.
5. I went to Spain two years ago and it was fantastic.

## TOP TIP

Nouns and adjectives are the easiest things to look up in the dictionary, and you will have one with you during the writing exam to help you on the day. Focus on learning verbs, connectors, etc., as in the table opposite – these are more difficult to work out for yourself.

Finally, to write your email conclusion, you can use the following phrase.

| | |
|---|---|
| *En espérant que ma candidature retienne votre attention, je vous prie d'agréer, cher Monsieur, chère Madame, l'expression de mes sentiments distingués.* | In the hope that my application is of interest to you, please accept, Sir/Madam, my regards. Yours faithfully, |
| *(nom)* | (name) |

## Exercise 8

Write all unseen/unpredictable bullet points from exercise 4 on pieces of paper and then draw any two from a hat. Then, using the introduction, the standard four bullet points, your two unseen bullet points and then conclusion, write out a sample essay in full.

# Preparing for reading

In this section, we'll look at how to approach the reading paper and how to ensure you secure each of those important marks.

Before you start a reading paper you should always have a strategy. This is one approach you could use:

1. Read the questions first.
2. Read the whole text quickly twice. Don't look up words; just get a general gist of what it's about.
3. Go back to the questions one by one to start to answer them. Highlight the key words in each question as you go – this will help direct you to the answers.
4. Check how many marks the question is worth.
5. Answer in sentences, ensuring that your answer makes sense in English and that you have all the information necessary for the number of marks. Remember that the answers will all be in the order that they appear in the text.

## Exercise 1

Understanding what kinds of things the questions are looking for will help you when you come to answer them yourself. To practise this, read the following text about Iceland and write six questions and then allocate marks depending on how much information it is possible to give in the answer. The first one is done for you.

### L'Islande

*L'Islande, une île volcanique aux frontières du cercle polaire, est un pays qui ne ressemble à aucun autre. Les anciens glaciers, les icebergs immenses, les volcans actifs et les sources chaudes nous donnent l'impression d'être plutôt sur la lune que sur Terre !*

*Si vous y êtes pendant l'hiver, les nuits sont claires et vous avez la possibilité de voir des aurores boréales\*. Ce phénomène naturel est un spectacle de nuit au cours duquel le ciel passe par toutes les couleurs imaginables : du rouge au vert, du bleu au rose. C'est une expérience impressionnante, émouvante et une vraie merveille de la nature qu'on vous encourage de voir au moins une fois dans votre vie !*

*Ce pays magnifique vous offrira de nombreuses expériences inoubliables dont l'une des plus extraordinaires est certainement d'observer les baleines. Voir ces animaux majestueux en pleine nature, c'est quelque chose que vous n'oublierez jamais.*

\* aurores boréales (English translation – Aurora Borealis) – another name for the Northern Lights

1. Where is Iceland located? Give one detail. (1)

Read the following passage and answer the questions in English.

### La musique et moi !

*Jacques, 15 ans, musicien*

*Ma mère est chanteuse et mon père joue de la batterie, donc j'ai grandi en écoutant de la musique tous les jours. A l'âge de quatre ans, j'ai commencé à apprendre à jouer du piano et il y a sept ans, j'ai commencé à jouer de la guitare.*

*Au collège, j'ai trouvé ça assez difficile de me concentrer sur mes études et j'ai souvent rêvé en classe que je jouais dans un stade devant une foule de cinquante mille personnes ! Pourtant, si jamais je deviens un musicien de rock célèbre, je préfère que ça soit grâce à mon talent et parce que j'écris des chansons que les gens adorent. Je n'ai pas envie d'être une de ces stars de la télé-réalité ou des concours de talents comme Z-Factor. Je suis avant tout musicien et je préfère garder un peu d'intégrité !*

1. What do Jacques' mum and dad do? (1)
2. When did he start to learn the guitar? (1)
3. What does Jacques dream about in class? (1)
4. What would he prefer to be famous for? (2)
5. Why would he not want to appear in a show like Z-Factor? (1)

When approaching a reading text, it is also very important that you include all the details. Never leave out words such as *très, assez* etc. or negatives such as *ne ... que, ne ... jamais* and *ne ... .rien* !

Read the text below and answer the questions in English.

1. Accoding to the article, when do pupils work best?
2. What does one pupil say is the impact on their work when a teacher is annoying?
3. What does Dr Elisabeth Gris say about getting on with teachers?
4. What is her advice for getting on with your teachers?
5. What do pupils think?

*Est-ce qu'il est possible d'être amis avec ses profs ?*

*Dans un sondage récent, huit élèves sur dix déclarent qu'ils travaillent mieux en cours quand ils s'entendent bien avec leurs profs.*

*'Si un prof m'énerve, je n'arrive pas à me concentrer et je n'ai plus envie de travailler' dit un élève.*

*Alors, comment faire pour avoir de bonnes relations avec ses profs ? 'Ce n'est pas toujours facile mais dans la vie, il faut apprendre à travailler avec des gens qu'on n'aime pas' affirme une experte en éducation, le Dr Elisabeth Gris.*

*Et ses conseils pour améliorer les relations avec les profs qu'on n'aime pas trop ?*

*'Premièrement, il ne faut jamais critiquer vos professeurs, ne pas vous plaindre si vous avez trop de travail et ne pas faire le clown en cours. Il faut toujours écouter ce qu'ils disent, sourire tout le temps et montrer aux professeurs que vous faites des efforts.'*

*Et les élèves, qu'est-ce qu'ils en pensent ? 'Il n'y a qu'un petit pourcentage de profs qui sont difficiles ou ennuyeux. En général, les cours sont assez intéressants.'*

*TOP TIP*

Before reading, thoroughly revise your key verbs. Watch out for irregular past participles, e.g devoir (to have to), dû, e.g. *J'ai dû* (I had to).

*TOP TIP*

Don't waste huge amounts of time trying to answer one particular point if you are really stuck. Give an answer you think might fit, star mark it so you remember which one it is and then move on. You can come back to it later and try again.

## Overall purpose of the text

The final question that you will have to answer in the reading and the listening paper is called the overall purpose of the text (OPT) question.

These are designed to test your comprehension of the text as a whole.

These will always be in multiple choice, tick-box format and are the final question in the reading paper.

*TOP TIP*

Leave the OPT question until last. At this point, you will have your best understanding of the whole text and so will be best placed to answer it correctly.

### Exercise 4

Go back through each of the reading texts from the 'Preparing for reading' section and then select the correct overall purpose of each text from the choices below. Pick three example sentences from the text which support your answer.

| Reading | 1 | 2 | 3 |
|---|---|---|---|
| *L'Islande* | To promote visiting Iceland? | To promote living in Iceland? | To promote studying in Iceland? |
| *La musique et moi !* | To discuss the role music has played in his relationships with his friends? | To talk about why music matters to young people? | To share his passion and experience of music? |
| *Est-ce qu'il est possible d'être amis avec ses profs ?* | To look at what makes a good teacher? | To examine relationships between teachers and students? | To discuss why teachers and students don't get on. |

# Preparing for listening

Lastly, let's look at some techniques which will help you get ready for listening.

Establishing a routine for listening is crucial in ensuring that you arrive prepared, calm and with a strategy. Here is one possible approach.

- Take a ruler into the exam and draw a line down the page, creating a section in each answer space where you can take notes.
- Read the questions before you listen to the text. Highlight key words and think about what you are listening for, e.g. Is it a time? You will hear the word **heure** if so.
- Predict the kinds of answers that might come up. Write a couple of quick notes.
- Check how many points you are looking for, e.g. two reasons.
- Listen to the recording and only take notes during this time.
- During the pause, go back and write your answers in full.
- Repeat the process for the second playing of the text.
- Cross out all of your notes when you are finished.

> ## TOP TIP
> To be good at listening, you simply need to recognise the vocabulary you know in its spoken form. The more you listen, the easier this becomes!

> ## TOP TIP
> The first text is always a presentation (one person) and the second text is always a conversation.

## Exercise 1

Now try the approach above when listening to the following text. Then answer the questions below.

Caroline is talking about a recent visit she made to Scotland, to visit her Scottish penpal, Fiona.

1. When did Caroline come to Scotland? (2)
2. What was she nervous about before coming? (Mention any one thing) (1)
3. Mention any one thing she particularly loved about Scotland. (1)
4. What one thing did she find difficult when she was here? (1)
5. What did she believe about Scotland before coming here? (1)
6. What two things does Caroline say she misses about Scotland? (2)

## Exercise 2

There is always an 'overall purpose of the text' question for the presentation part of the listening. It will always be the final question and is a tick box answer worth 1 point. Listen to the text again and then choose the correct answer below:

What does Caroline mainly talk about?

> 1. Her experiences and impressions of Scotland.
> 2. The difficulties she encountered on her trip.
> 3. The differences she noticed between French and Scottish culture.

## Exercise 3

How many of the questions did you get right? Go back over the text and read and listen to it at the same time. Take a note of the vocabulary you didn't quite get and then listen to it all again without reading it this time.

### TOP TIP
You don't need to understand every single word. The trick with listening is to be able to pick out the key details.

### TOP TIP
Listen, listen and listen again. The more you listen, the more accustomed you will become to listening to French. Save listening texts on a playlist at home and listen to them over and over again.

## Conversation

The second part of the listening assessment is always a conversation between two people on a different topic from the presentation. You will have 1 minute to look over your questions again and go through the routine as outlined at the start of this chapter. The conversation is worth 12 points.

## Exercise 4

Listen to Moran being interviewed on a radio station about his past times and answer the questions in English.

1. What examples of creative past times does Moran give? Mention any two things. (2)
2. How often does he do sport? (1)
3. What kinds of sports does he enjoy? Mention any two things. (2)
4. What part-time job does he do? (1)
5. Moran talks about his weekend. Tick the statements that are correct. (2)

---

1. He likes to rest on Saturdays. ☐
2. He goes to the cinema with his family. ☐
3. He's a fan of comedy films. ☐
4. There is a good cinema near his house. ☐

---

6. What does he do on Sundays? (2)
7. What is he planning to do when he leaves school? (2)

# Key vocabulary

The vocabulary in this chapter covers some of the key additional vocabulary that you should know. Pay attention to the top tips and exercises, take it bit-by-bit and make it your goal to know each of these sets of vocabulary inside out!

## Time phrases

| | |
|---|---|
| tous les jours | every day |
| chaque semaine | each week |
| quinze jours | a fortnight (2 weeks) |
| hier | yesterday |
| demain | tomorrow |
| l'année prochaine | next year |
| l'année dernière | last year |
| il y a deux ans | two years ago |
| quelquefois | sometimes |
| plusieurs fois | several times |
| une fois par semaine | once a week |
| pendant | during |
| avant/après | before/after |

### Exercise 1

Write one sentence for each of the expressions of time above, e.g. *Je joue au foot tous les jours*.

## Expressions of quantity

| | |
|---|---|
| un peu de | a little of |
| beaucoup de | a lot of |
| plusieurs | several |
| plein de | a lot of |
| trop de | too much of |
| quelques | some |
| une moitié | a half |
| demi | half |
| un quart de | a quarter of |
| moins de | less of |
| plus de | more of |
| encore | more |
| assez de | enough of |

**TOP TIP**

Expressions of quantity are usually followed by **de** in French, e.g. *beaucoup de, assez de*, etc.

### Exercise 2

Think of things you have or would like and then use them to create '*Je voudrais cards*'. Include the expressions of quantity on the cards, e.g. *Je voudrais encore des vêtements*.

# Question words

| | |
|---|---|
| comment ? | how? |
| combien de ? | how many? |
| quand ? | when? |
| où ? | where? |
| qui ? | who? |
| quel/quelle/quels/quelles ? | which? |
| quoi ? | what? |
| pourquoi ? | why? |
| à quelle heure ? | at what time? |

**Exercise 3**

Decide which question word is missing from each of the sentences below.

1. *Il y a _____ personnes ici ce soir ?*
2. *_____ est le stade de foot ?*
3. *_____ est-ce que la fête commence ? A _____ heure ?*
4. *Ton meilleur ami, c'est _____ ?*
5. *_____ préfères-tu les voitures françaises ?*

**TOP TIP**

Words like **où** are small but important – make sure you know them!

# Prepositions

| | |
|---|---|
| environ | about |
| en haut | above |
| sous | below |
| après | after |
| contre | against |
| autour de | around |
| au bout de | at the end of |
| derrière | behind |
| entre | between |
| partout | everywhere |
| loin de | far from |
| dans | in |
| dedans | inside |
| près de | near |
| à côté de | beside |

Some of the prepositions in the table above are followed by **de**. The **de** changes to agree with the gender of the noun that follows. For example:

| de + masculine singular | du | A côté du château | Beside the castle |
|---|---|---|---|
| de + feminine singular | de la | A côté de la gare | Beside the station |
| de + feminine singular + vowel | de l' | A côté de l'église | Beside the church |
| de + plural | des | A côté des magasins | Beside the shops |

Go around your home/bedroom and make signs on sticky notes saying what is where, e.g. *'La télé est sur la table'*. Highlight the prepositions and leave them there as a revision reminder. See if you can use all the prepositions from the list opposite. Be sure to seek the permission of your parents/guardians before carrying out this activity!

## Connectors

The following words are useful if you are looking to extend your sentences and make them more interesting and complex.

| | |
|---|---|
| *et* | and |
| *aussi* | also |
| *parce que* | because |
| *car* | because |
| *mais* | but |
| *cependant* | however |
| *pourtant* | however |
| *néanmoins* | nonetheless |
| *même si* | even if |
| *enfin* | finally |
| *si* | if |
| *ou* | or |
| *puisque* | since |
| *donc* | so |
| *alors* | so |
| *puis* | then |
| *ensuite* | then |

Use the connectors above to link the beginning and ends of the following sentences.

1.  *Je fais du footing trois fois par semaine _____ j'essaie de garder la forme.*
2.  *Le film était très émouvant _____ j'ai pleuré un peu à la fin.*
3.  *Il a acheté une voiture _____ trois semaines plus tard il a _____ acheté une maison !*
4.  *J'ai goûté les escargots _____ j'essaie d'être aventureux !*
5.  *Il est sympa _____ il est un peu égoïste parfois.*

## Modifiers

| | |
|---|---|
| *très* | very |
| *assez* | quite |
| *un peu* | a bit |
| *vraiment* | really |
| *trop* | too |

Adapt the following sentences to include one of the modifiers from the table opposite.

1. *Je serai _____ content(e) quand les examens seront finis !*
2. *Ma mère est _____ gentille mais elle peut être _____ sévère de temps en temps.*
3. *Les arbres dans mon jardins sont _____ grands.*
4. *A mon avis, il faut toujours être _____ respectueux de l'environnement.*

# Key verbs

The following verbs are those which tend to be the most common and are therefore a good selection to focus on knowing. You're not expected to know them all off by heart, but make sure you can recognise their infinitives, their future stems and the past participles.

| Infinintive | English | Perfect tense | Imperfect | Future |
|---|---|---|---|---|
| *aller* | | *je suis allé(e)* | *j'allais* | *j'irai* |
| *avoir* | | *j'ai eu* | *j'avais* | *j'aurai* |
| *connaître* | | *j'ai connu* | *je connaissais* | *je connaîtrai* |
| *comprendre* | | *j'ai compris* | *je comprenais* | *je comprendrai* |
| *être* | | *j'ai été* | *j'étais* | *je serai* |
| *devoir* | | *j'ai dû* | *je devais* | *je devrai* |
| *dire* | | *j'ai dit* | *je disais* | *je dirai* |
| *donner* | | *j'ai donné* | *je donnais* | *je donnerai* |
| *faire* | | *j'ai fait* | *je faisais* | *je ferai* |
| *mettre* | | *j'ai mis* | *je mettais* | *je mettrai* |
| *parler* | | *j'ai parlé* | *je parlais* | *je parlerai* |
| *perdre* | | *j'ai perdu* | *je perdais* | *je perdrai* |
| *prendre* | | *j'ai pris* | *je prenais* | *je prendrai* |
| *savoir* | | *j'ai su* | *je savais* | *je saurai* |
| *trouver* | | *j'ai trouvé* | *je trouvais* | *je trouverai* |
| *venir* | | *je suis venu(e)* | *je venais* | *je viendrai* |
| *vivre* | | *j'ai vécu* | *je vivais* | *je vivrai* |
| *voir* | | *j'ai vu* | *je voyais* | *je verrai* |
| *vouloir* | | *j'ai voulu* | *je voulais* | *je voudrai* |

Go through the verbs above and add the English translations to the table. Then pick any five of the verbs and conjugate them in full in the present, perfect, imperfect, future and conditional tenses. An example is done for you below.

| *Voir* – to see | | | | |
|---|---|---|---|---|
| **Present** | **Perfect** | **Imperfect** | **Future** | **Conditional** |
| *je vois* | *j'ai vu* | *je voy**ais*** | *je verr**ai*** | *je verr**ais*** |
| *tu vois* | *tu as vu* | *tu voy**ais*** | *tu verr**as*** | *tu verr**ais*** |
| *il/elle/on voit* | *il/elle/on a vu* | *il/elle/on voy**ait*** | *il/elle/on verr**a*** | *il/elle/on verr**ait*** |
| *nous voyons* | *nous avons vu* | *nous voy**ions*** | *nous ver**rons*** | *nous verr**ions*** |
| *vous voyez* | *vous avez vu* | *vous voy**iez*** | *vous verr**ez*** | *vous verr**iez*** |
| *ils/elles voient* | *ils/elles ont vu* | *ils/elles voy**aient*** | *ils/elles verr**ont*** | *ils/elles verr**aient*** |

# Numbers in French

| | | | |
|---|---|---|---|
| 0 | *zéro* | 71 | *soixante et onze* |
| 1 | *un* | 72 | *soixante-douze* |
| 2 | *deux* | 73 | *soixante-treize* |
| 3 | *trois* | 74 | *soixante-quatorze* |
| 4 | *quatre* | 75 | *soixante-quinze* |
| 5 | *cinq* | 76 | *soixante-seize* |
| 6 | *six* | 77 | *soixante-dix-sept* |
| 7 | *sept* | 78 | *soixante-dix-huit* |
| 8 | *huit* | 79 | *soixante-dix-neuf* |
| 9 | *neuf* | 80 | *quatre-vingts* |
| 10 | *dix* | 81 | *quatre-vingt-un* |
| 11 | *onze* | 82 | *quatre-vingt-deux* |
| 12 | *douze* | 83 | *quatre-vingt-trois* |
| 13 | *treize* | 84 | *quatre-vingt-quatre* |
| 14 | *quatorze* | 85 | *quatre-vingt-cinq* |
| 15 | *quinze* | 86 | *quatre-vingt-six* |
| 16 | *seize* | 87 | *quatre-vingt-sept* |
| 17 | *dix-sept* | 88 | *quatre-vingt-huit* |
| 18 | *dix-huit* | 89 | *quatre-vingt-neuf* |
| 19 | *dix-neuf* | 90 | *quatre-vingt-dix* |
| 20 | *vingt* | 91 | *quatre-vingt-onze* |
| 21 | *vingt et un* | 92 | *quatre-vingt-douze* |
| 22 | *vingt-deux* | 93 | *quatre-vingt-treize* |
| 23 | *vingt-trois* | 94 | *quatre-vingt-quatorze* |
| 24 | *vingt-quatre* | 95 | *quatre-vingt-quinze* |
| 25 | *vingt-cinq* | 96 | *quatre-vingt-seize* |
| 26 | *vingt-six* | 97 | *quatre-vingt-dix-sept* |
| 27 | *vingt-sept* | 98 | *quatre-vingt-dix-huit* |
| 28 | *vingt-huit* | 99 | *quatre-vingt-dix-neuf* |
| 29 | *vingt-neuf* | 100 | *cent* |
| 30 | *trente* | 200 | *deux cents* |
| 31 | *trente et un* | 201 | *deux cent un* |
| 32 | *trente-deux* | 1000 | *mille* |
| 40 | *quarante* | 2000 | *deux mille* |
| 50 | *cinquante* | 2500 | *deux mille cinq cents* |
| 60 | *soixante* | 1,000,000 | *un million* |
| 70 | *soixante-dix* | 2,000,000 | *deux millions* |

*TOP TIP*

Focus on learning the numbers you find most difficult. Quite often these are the numbers in the teens (e.g. *douze, treize, quatorze, quinze, seize* etc.) and the numbers greater than 60. Listen to them and practise saying them over and over until you've got them!

### Exercise 8

Write the numbers 1–9. Listen to the following French phone numbers and write them down as you listen.

### Exercise 9

Read back through the numbers and try saying them yourself now. Time yourself doing all 10 and see how fast you are!

# Society

## Friends

### Exercise 3 – page 17

*Adèle :* *Tu aimes nos camarades de classe, Sadiq ?*

*Sadiq :* *Oui, je m'entends bien avec la plupart des personnes de la classe. Et toi ?*

*Adèle :* *Oui, en général, je m'entends bien avec mes camarades de classe. Oh, sauf avec Christophe. On ne s'entend pas bien. Il me critique tout le temps.*

*Sadiq :* *Christophe ? Moi, je m'entends bien avec Christophe. On ne se dispute jamais. Et Sophie ? Est-ce que tu t'entends bien avec Sophie ? Sophie et moi on rigole bien tous les deux.*

*Adèle :* *Sophie est une bonne amie. Elle a une bonne influence sur moi.*

*Sadiq :* *C'est vrai. A mon avis, André a beaucoup d'humour.*

*Adèle :* *Oui, il est très drôle. On discute souvent au téléphone et on s'envoie beaucoup de SMS.*

*Sadiq :* *Je discute de tout avec Max. C'est quelqu'un de très fiable et je peux me confier à lui.*

*Adèle :* *Moi aussi, j'ai beaucoup de choses en commun avec Max. On a les mêmes goûts.*

*Sadiq :* *Oui, il est super cool.*

*Adèle :* *Et toi, tu es cool aussi, Sadiq !*

*Sadiq :* *Moi ? Oh merci, Adèle ! On s'entend bien, toi et moi.*

*Adèle :* *Oui, très bien !*

## Sport and exercise

### Exercise 1 – page 23

*La ville de Gardez-la-forme se trouve à la montagne et au bord d'un lac. Elle est donc très bien située pour les sports nautiques et les sports d'hiver. 23 personnes sur 100 aiment pratiquer des sports nautiques comme la voile. Et quand la neige, arrive les sports d'hiver sont aussi très appréciés. 36 personnes sur 100 aiment faire du ski et 15 personnes sur 100 aiment faire du surf des neiges. Le surf des neiges est surtout populaire chez les jeunes !*

*Par ailleurs, il y a d'autres sports qui sont aussi très populaires. 45 personnes sur 100 aiment le foot mais on ne sait pas s'ils préfèrent jouer ou simplement regarder ! L'équitation est assez appréciée : 7 personnes sur 100 aiment faire du cheval. 48 personnes sur 100 aiment faire du vélo ou du VTT en été et 10 personnes sur 100 aiment jouer au golf. Sachez enfin que la randonnée est très populaire dans cette ville et pratiquée par 67 % de ses habitants.*

## New technologies

### Exercise 2 – page 31

*Guillaume :* *Christine, ma belle, c'est bientôt ton anniversaire : tu auras soixante ans ! Un anniversaire à fêter tout particulièrement ! Qu'est-ce que tu veux comme cadeau ? Je pensais à un joli pull en laine ou à un flacon de parfum peut-être ? Ou sinon, je pourrais t'offrir un bon d'achat pour ton magasin préféré ?*

*Christine :* *Ah non, chéri. Tu ne me connais pas ? ! Tu sais bien que je préfère toujours les nouvelles technologies ! J'ai vu un nouvel ordinateur portable avec un écran tactile par exemple. Et je ne supporte plus mon téléphone portable ; je ne peux pas passer ni recevoir des appels vidéo ni accéder à Internet, c'est complètement démodé ! Il me faut un smartphone !*

**Guillaume :** *D'accord, d'accord ... mais tu sais bien que les nouvelles technologies coûtent très chères et, chérie, les gens passent trop de temps sur Internet !*

**Christine :** *C'est vrai, mais à mon avis, les technologies améliorent nos vies. Je peux trouver toute l'information que je veux, chatter avec mes amis, parler avec la famille à l'étranger, organiser les vacances ou faire du shopping en ligne. C'est génial !*

**Guillaume :** *Vacances, shopping, encore beaucoup d'argent ! Bon, ce n'est pas grave ; pour toi, parce que je t'aime, je t'achèterai une nouvelle tablette alors !*

**Christine :** *Oh c'est super, merci, Guillaume ! Je voudrais le tout dernier modèle, s'il te plaît. Vaut mieux être à jour !*

**Guillaume :** *Oh oui, bien sûr, le tout dernier modèle ... d'accord chérie, pour toi, rien n'est trop beau ! Mais je vais t'offrir ce cadeau à condition que tu ne l'utilises pas plus de deux heures par soir. Il est important qu'on continue de discuter en face-à-face.*

**Christine :** *D'accord ! Il n'y a pas de problème, chéri !*

# Global languages

## Exercise 2 – page 33

### Annas, 17 ans, Fès, Maroc.

*Salut, je m'appelle Annas et j'habite à Fès au Maroc. Le Maroc se trouve dans le nord-ouest de l'Afrique sur la côte méditerranéenne. C'est un pays arabe et il y a deux langues officielles : l'arabe et le berbère\*. Moi, je parle quatre langues, en fait. Je parle l'arabe et le français à l'école et j'apprends l'espagnol aussi. Quand je suis chez moi et avec ma famille, je parle le berbère. C'est notre langue locale, je la parle avec mes parents et mes grands-parents en particulier. Pour moi, c'est un grand honneur de pouvoir parler plusieurs langues. Une fois que j'aurai fini mes études, je voudrais travailler dans le commerce. J'aimerais donc apprendre aussi l'anglais. Pour nous, c'est normal de parler plusieurs langues et ça nous permet de réussir dans la vie.*

\* berbère means Berber

### Ryuichi, 15 ans, Nagasaki, Japon

*Bonjour, je m'appelle Ryuichi et je suis japonais. J'habite dans une grande ville qui s'appelle Nagasaki et se trouve dans le sud du Japon. Au Japon, on parle le japonais. C'est une langue qui est assez difficile à écrire. On doit beaucoup pratiquer à l'école et on met du temps à maîtriser notre langue ! J'apprends aussi l'anglais depuis l'école maternelle, depuis l'âge de trois ans. J'aime parler anglais et à mon avis, il est essentiel de savoir parler au moins deux langues étrangères. Puisque je voudrais travailler dans l'industrie automobile, j'ai commencé à apprendre l'allemand. Je ne sais pas si je vais travailler pour une entreprise allemande, mais je préférerais être familiarisé avec cette langue, comme ça j'aurai plus de chance si jamais j'ai l'occasion de postuler pour un poste chez un fabricant allemand. Au minimum, mes compétences linguistiques montreront que je suis intelligent et travailleur.*

### Steffie, 16 ans, Berlin, Allemagne

*Salut ! Je m'appelle Steffie et je viens de Berlin, la capitale de l'Allemagne. Ici, à Berlin, la plupart des gens sont bilingues. Nous parlons tous l'allemand et beaucoup d'Allemands parlent aussi l'anglais. Moi, je parle allemand à la maison et avec mes amis, et j'apprends l'anglais au lycée. J'apprends aussi le russe et je sais un peu de français. Pour moi, il est important de parler plusieurs langues pour mieux comprendre les étrangers et le monde.*

# The environment

## Exercise 3 – page 41

***Mme Vert :*** *Bonjour, monsieur Le Gaspillage. Vous avez noté que nous avons des bacs de recyclage dans la rue maintenant.*

***M. Le Gaspillage :*** *Les bacs de recyclage dans la rue ! Quelle horreur ! Je ne fais jamais de recyclage. Je ne recycle rien ! Je ne m'intéresse pas du tout à l'environnement.*

***Mme Vert :*** *Oh monsieur, c'est une attitude méprisable ! Je ne mets plus rien dans la poubelle, j'essaie de tout recycler ! Et est-ce que vous économisez l'énergie à la maison ?*

***M. le Gaspillage :*** *Economiser l'énergie ? ! J'économise l'énergie quand je ne fais rien ! Je n'éteins jamais les lumières.*

***Mme Vert :*** *C'est vraiment incroyable. Moi, quand je fais les courses, je n'achète que des produits bios. Et vous ?*

***M. Le Gaspillage :*** *Vous plaisantez, madame ! Au contraire, je n'achète que des produits non-bios ! Je n'achète que des produits non-recyclables, non-bios et mauvais pour l'environnement !*

***Mme Vert :*** *Monsieur, vous n'avez aucun respect pour notre planète !*

***M. Le Gaspillage :*** *Oui, c'est vrai. Sauf que je ne prends que les transports en commun, je ne prends jamais la voiture pour les trajets courts.*

***Mme Vert :*** *Oh bravo, monsieur ! Ce n'est pas beaucoup, mais c'est mieux que rien !*

# Learning

## Learning in other subjects

### Exercise 2 – page 50

1. *Personnellement, je préfère les matières logiques comme les sciences et les maths.*
2. *A mon avis, en anglais, il y a beaucoup de devoirs. Il y a un peu trop de devoirs en fait.*
3. *Je trouve que les matières scientifiques sont ennuyeuses et trop compliquées.*
4. *La musique m'intéresse plus que la géographie. En général, je préfères les matières créatives.*
5. *Il faut dire que je suis faible en histoire.*

## Preparing for exams

### Exercise 1 – page 53

*Sara : Tu as des examens bientôt, Jean ?*

*Jean : Oui, c'est l'horreur, j'ai beaucoup de révisions à faire !*

*Sara : Tu as des examens en quelles matières ?*

*Jean : J'ai des examens en EPS, anglais, chimie, maths et histoire.*

*Sara : Et un examen en français aussi ?*

*Jean : Oui, j'ai oublié ! Un examen en français aussi ! Ça fait six matières au total ! C'est trop !*

*Sara : Et comment est-ce que tu révises ?*

*Jean : D'abord, j'établis des horaires de révisions et puis j'essaie de m'y atteler.*

*Sara : Tu fais combien d'heures par jour ?*

*Jean : En générale, je fais environ dix heures par jour. Je fais quatre heures le matin, trois heures l'après-midi et trois heures le soir.*

*Sara : C'est beaucoup ! Tu n'es pas fatigué ?*

*Jean : Si, et c'est ennuyeux mais je voudrais réussir mes examens et avoir de bonnes notes, donc il faut que je travaille beaucoup.*

*Sara : Tu préfères travailler le matin ou le soir ?*

*Jean : Je préfère travailler le matin mais à mon avis, les deux sont pénibles !*

*Sara : Est-ce-que tu écoutes de la musique pendant que tu travailles ?*

*Jean : J'écoute toujours de la musique quand je travaille. La musique me détend et les révisions sont plus amusantes lorsqu'on en écoute !*

*Sara : C'est vrai ! OK, je te laisse travailler ! Bonne chance, Jean, bon courage !*

*Jean : Merci, Sara ! C'est gentil.*

## Learner responsibilities

### Exercise 3 – page 57

*Lucas : Est-ce que je suis une bon élève ? Je ne sais pas, mais je fais toujours mes devoirs et j'écoute toujours le prof en classe. Je me déconcentre un peu mais en général, je suis sage et je travaille bien.*

*Alain : J'ai beaucoup de respect pour les professeurs parce qu'ils travaillent dur pour que les cours soient intéressants et agréables. Je m'entends bien avec les profs et, par conséquent, je travaille bien et j'essaie d'être bien organisé.*

*Jennie :* L'école ne m'intéresse pas du tout, c'est donc un défi pour moi de bien me comporter tout le temps. J'ai l'habitude d'oublier mes devoirs et de parler en classe. Je ne suis pas bien organisée en général donc je perds souvent mon cahier. Je n'y peux rien !

## Employability

### Exercise 2 – page 59

*Angela :* Je travaille dans un supermarché trois jours par semaine. Je travaille le samedi, le dimanche et le lundi après l'école. Je commence le week-end à huit heures et je finis à dix-sept heures. C'est une longue journée, mais je travaille surtout avec les clients donc je m'amuse en leur parlant pour faire passer le temps. Je gagne 5 euros de l'heure. C'est assez bien payé à mon avis. Est-ce que j'aime mon petit boulot ? Oui, ce n'est pas mal et j'aime rencontrer des gens.

*Guilhem :* J'ai la malchance d'avoir un petit boulot dans un magasin et je déteste ça. Je dois travailler cinq jours par semaine (du lundi au vendredi) entre dix-huit heures et vingt-deux heures. Ça ne me laisse pas beaucoup de temps pour faire mes devoirs, ce qui me pose des problèmes pour l'école. J'ai des tâches pénibles à faire tel que le nettoyage. Pourtant, c'est très bien payé : je gagne 7 euros 50 de l'heure. En gros, je dirais que je déteste mon petit boulot mais j'aime l'argent donc je continue de le faire.

## Work and CVs

### Exercise 3 – page 63

*Professeur :* Alors Caty, qu'est-ce que tu vas faire comme stage ?

*Elève :* Je vais travailler chez un médecin.

*Professeur :* Ah, c'est beaucoup de responsabilité ! Où est-ce que tu vas travailler ?

*Elève :* Oui, mais je suis une personne très responsable quand même ! Je vais travailler au centre-ville.

*Professeur :* Ah bon, c'est très bien ! Et qu'est-ce que tu vas faire au travail ?

*Elève :* Je vais classer les dossiers des patients.

*Professeur :* Tu vas commencer à quelle heure ?

*Elève :* Je vais commencer à huit heures et quart. C'est un peu trop tôt pour moi !

*Professeur :* Comment est-ce que tu vas aller au travail ?

*Elève :* En fait, le cabinet médical n'est pas trop loin de chez moi donc je vais y aller à pied.

*Professeur :* Qu'est-ce que tu vas porter au travail ?

*Elève :* A mon avis, il est important d'être bien habillé, donc je vais porter une jupe et un chemisier.

*Professeur :* Alors je te souhaite bon courage et bonne chance !

*Elève :* Merci, monsieur !

# Culture

## Aspects of other countries

### Exercise 2 – page 77

1. *Il y a environ 26000 boulangeries en France et on estime que 98% des Français mangent du pain tous les jours !*
2. *Il y a plus de 5000 restaurants à Paris.*
3. *Les Français mangent l'équivalent de 25 kg de fromage par personne et par an.*
4. *Il y a plus de 300 sortes de fromages différents en France.*

### Exercise 4 – page 77

*Les grands événements de l'histoire de France ? Oh, voyons, il y en a beaucoup !*

*La Révolution française a commencé en 1789 et s'est terminée en 1799.*

*Le roi de France, Louis XVI et sa femme, Marie-Antoinette, ont été exécutés pendant la Révolution. Louis XVI d'abord, le 21 juin 1793, et puis Marie-Antoinette, neuf mois plus tard, le 16 octobre 1793.*

*Les guerres napoléoniennes sont une série de batailles et de guerres qui ont eu lieu entre la France et la Grande-Bretagne entre 1799 et 1815. La dernière bataille est celle de Waterloo qui a eu lieu le dimanche 18 juin 1815 à Waterloo en Belgique.*

*La Première Guerre mondiale, entre 1914 et 1918, puis la Seconde Guerre mondiale, entre 1939 et 1945, ont été toutes les deux très difficiles pour la France parce qu'une grande partie des combats se sont déroulés en France.*

## Literature of France

### Exercise 4 – page 84

*J'adore lire et j'essaie de lire au moins un roman par mois. J'aime bien les romans classiques et les histoires de science-fiction comme 'Vingt mille lieues sous les mers de l'écrivain Jules Verne. J'aime aussi son livre célèbre, 'Le Tour du monde en quatre-vingts jours'. C'est un livre qui a eu beaucoup d'influence sur moi, il m'a donné envie de voyager et de prendre une année sabbatique ! Sinon, je suis également fan de romans d'aventures et historiques comme Les Trois Mousquetaires et Le Comte de Monte-Cristo. Je trouve que les intrigues de ces romans sont très bien construites et les deux romans tiennent le lecteur en haleine !*

*Il y a bien sûr, des livres français classiques pour les jeunes comme 'Le Petit Nicolas' ou 'Le Petit Prince'. Parmi les deux, j'ai toujours préféré 'Le Petit Nicolas' parce que je pouvais m'identifier au personnage principal, Nicolas, et parce que les histoires racontées dans ce livre m'ont toujours fait rire.*

## Television

### Exercise 2 – page 89

**Jean :** *Je suis accro à la télé et j'adore tous les genres d'émissions mais je pense que je préfère les émissions de sport et les séries américaines. Je sais que je regarde trop la télé et comme j'ai une télé dans ma chambre, je la regarde jusqu'à ce que je m'endorme ! Je trouve qu'en général, la télé française est très bien faite mais il y a un peu trop d'informations et de politique. C'est un peu trop sérieux. On regarde la télé pour se détendre, pas pour regarder des choses graves quand même.*

**Béa :** *Quand je la regarde, je regarde des comédies et des fois, des émissions de variétés comme Danse avec les Stars. Je regarde très peu la télé. Je préfère être en plein air plutôt que de rester enfermé chez soi, cloué devant la télé. Je ne supporte pas les gens qui regardent la télé et qui ne font que ça ! Si tu me demandes ce que j'en pense, je te dirais que ça les rend paresseux !*

**Paul :** *J'aime regarder la télé et je préfère les séries policières et les thrillers. Généralement, je regarde la télé le soir, une fois que j'ai fini mes devoirs. C'est bien pour se vider la tête et ça me fait du bien de penser à autre chose. La vie, c'est stressant et la télé me détend !*

# Preparing for assessment
## Preparing for listening

### Exercise 1 – page 107

*Bonjour, je m'appelle Caroline et j'ai quinze ans. Je suis française et j'habite dans le sud-ouest de la France, près de Toulouse. Il y a deux ans, au mois de juillet, j'ai rendu visite à ma correspondante, Fiona, en Ecosse.*

*Avant de voyager en Ecosse, j'avais très peur parce que je ne parlais pas très bien l'anglais et j'ai entendu dire que l'accent écossais était difficile à comprendre et que les gens parlaient très rapidement ! Pourtant, quand je suis arrivée, Fiona m'a aidée et j'ai appris beaucoup d'anglais !*

*L'Ecosse est un pays très beau et pittoresque ; j'ai surtout adoré les paysages. De plus, les gens étaient tous très sympas.*

*Il y avait, bien sûr, des difficultés de temps en temps, mais le plus difficile pour moi c'était le temps qu'il faisait là-bas. Il pleuvait tous les jours et il faisait froid ! Je ne pourrais pas y habiter ! Je suis habituée au beau temps en France !*

*Avant de visiter l'Ecosse, je croyais que tous les hommes portaient des kilts et que tout le monde mangeait du haggis ! En fait, ce n'est pas vrai !*

*Maintenant que je suis de retour en France, il y a certaines choses écossaises qui me manque. Ma correspondante et sa famille bien sûr, parce qu'ils étaient vraiment gentils ; et deuxièmement, les monuments historiques et l'architecture qui m'ont beaucoup impressionnés pendant mon séjour en Ecosse.*

### Exercise 4 – page 108

***Interviewer :*** *Bonjour, Moran, ça va ?*

***Moran :*** *Oui, ça va très bien, merci. Merci de m'avoir invité à venir vous parler aujourd'hui.*

***Interviewer :*** *Alors on discute de passe-temps. Qu'est-ce que vous aimez faire pendant votre temps libre, Moran ?*

***Moran :*** *J'aime les passe-temps créatifs. Par exemple, je joue de la guitare classique et j'apprends à jouer de la trompette. J'aime aussi le dessin, je trouve que ça me détend.*

***Interviewer :*** *Et vous aimez faire du sport ?*

***Moran :*** *Oui, j'adore ça. Je suis quelqu'un de sportif : je fais du sport au moins une fois par jour.*

***Interviewer :*** *Vous pratiquez quels sports exactement ?*

***Moran :*** *Je joue au foot dans notre équipe au lycée et j'aime faire du footing aussi. Ça me maintient en forme pour les grands matchs ! J'ai acheté un VTT récemment, donc c'est ma nouvelle passion !*

***Interviewer :*** *Ça coûte cher ! Vous avez un petit boulot ?*

***Moran :*** *Oui, je livre des journaux le matin avant l'école.*

***Interviewer :*** *Waouh, vous avez une vie très active ! Et qu'est-ce que vous faites le week-end ?*

***Moran :*** *Le samedi, j'essaie de me reposer un peu et de passer du temps avec mes amis et ma petite-amie. Nous allons souvent au cinéma le samedi soir. Je suis fan des films d'horreur ! Il y a un très bon cinéma près de chez moi.*

***Interviewer :*** *Et le dimanche ? Qu'est-ce que vous faites le dimanche ?*

***Moran :*** *Le dimanche, je prends un bon petit-déjeuner avec ma famille et puis je révise mes cours. J'ai des examens bientôt, alors je dois travailler pour réussir.*

*Interviewer :* C'est très sage. Qu'est-ce que vous voulez faire après le lycée ?

*Moran :* Je voudrais aller à la fac pour étudier le droit et le chinois. J'espère passer un an en Chine pour apprendre la langue.

*Interviewer :* Je vous souhaite beaucoup de chance alors et bon courage !

*Moran :* Merci, au revoir !

## Exercise 8 – page 114
1. 04 76 23 47 89
2. 03 21 12 15 67
3. 01 34 56 87 22
4. 02 25 49 13 06
5. 06 98 17 36 28
6. 05 59 65 15 91
7. 06 10 01 18 99
8. 01 02 32 14 44
9. 09 45 04 69 77

LECKIE
the education publisher
for Scotland

# National 5
# FRENCH

For SQA 2019 and beyond

**Practice Papers**

Eleanor McLellan

# Top exam tips

## The Writing Assignment

The Writing Assignment is worth 20 marks altogether and should be between 120 – 200 words in length and will cover any of the themes of Society, Learning or Culture. You will have a chance to write, correct and redraft this in class before it is finally submitted to the SQA for marking. Use this opportunity to produce your best work, ensuring that it is well-presented, written carefully with attention to accuracy and detail. Go beyond the basic and take the chance to shine but always make sure that you know what you are writing is correct!

To support your writing, you can use:

- The assignment question in English.

- Grammar reference notes e.g. verb tables or notes on forming the perfect/imperfect tense.

- A bilingual dictionary.

- Wordlists or vocabulary lists.

- Writing improvement codes or notes.

- Draft versions or notes.

You cannot use materials such as text books, online resources, lists of phrases or jotters.

When answering the questions, you don't need to answer all the bullet points, however, it's worth noting that the scenario probably will give you a natural essay structure. Consider the following when writing:

- Ensure you have a clear and interesting introduction.

- Write in paragraphs to structure your writing and develop your ideas.

- Include your opinions using interesting phrases e.g. **à mon avis, je pense que, en ce qui me concerne,** etc.

- Vary your sentence length and use connectors e.g. **mais, et, parce que, car,** etc.

- Check for gender (**un, une, des, le, la, les**), verb, tense, adjective agreement, plurals, etc.

- Ensure your spelling is accurate.

- Go further than the basic phrases! Find some fantastic French to make your writing shine!

The Assignment is a great opportunity to really show what you can do. Most of all, work hard and do your best!

# The Reading exam

In the National 5 Reading exam, there will be three texts worth 10 marks each. You have to answer the questions in English. When you are given the paper, you should work through the three questions in order. They will be on different contexts you have covered in class – Society, Learning, Employability and Culture. The context that is not covered in the Reading paper will be the subject of the Listening exam. You are given 1 hour and 30 minutes for the Reading and Writing paper. You should try to complete the Reading questions in an hour, leaving 30 minutes for the Writing question. That means you have 20 minutes to answer each question.

Follow these steps to complete the paper and maximise your marks.

## When you open your question paper:

- First read the information in English at the top of the question, as this will give you an idea of what the question is about.

- It is not usual for texts in the National 5 Reading exam to have a heading. However, if there is a heading, it will be in French. Work out what it means, as it will help you to understand what the question is about.

- Disregard the picture. Your answers will always come from the text – the picture is only to make it look nice!

- Skim read the passage.

- Skim read the questions.

Up to this point you should not have opened the dictionary! Remember, you have to answer the questions – not translate all of the passage.

## When you start answering the questions:

- Don't start with the passage – start by looking at the questions in English.

- Look at each question in turn and mark where the answer can be found in the text, using a highlighter or underlining the relevant part of the text.

- Marking where each answer is cuts down on the amount of work you have to do. Most importantly, if there is a question you can't find the answer to it is often in any unmarked sections of the paper. This again helps you to pinpoint the relevant parts of the text and allows you to complete the paper with the highest mark.

- There are often clue words in the question (in English) that lead you to where the answer is (in French). These clue words are usually words that are similar in French and English, or they are words that should be familiar to you in French.

- Work out the meaning of the relevant part of the text to enable you to answer the question. Think about individual words, but also think about the sentence as a whole. You may be able to work out tricky words from the context of the sentence.

- It is only at this point that you should think about looking up any words you don't know in the dictionary. Remember to read the whole definition and choose the one that fits the answer best.

- When you are answering the questions, make sure that you put in as much detail as possible and that you actually answer the question.

- Stick to what the information in the text says – don't add in extra information you might know on the subject or draw conclusions from the information in the passage. You must write down what the answer is from the French in the passage.

## When you have written your answers:

- Read them over to make sure that what you have written makes sense in English. The person marking your paper will always look for the positives in your answers, but they must be able to understand what you have written.

Mark any gaps you have in your answers so that you can go back to try to complete them when you are finished. It is easy to forget at the end of the paper that you have missed out a couple of questions. If you highlight them in some way – it could be by circling the numbers of the questions you have missed out – then you will remember to go over them as you look over your paper.

## 'What is the purpose?' question

- The last question in the last passage will ask you what the purpose of the passage was.

- You will have to choose from three options and tick the box you think gives the correct answer.

- This question is not designed to trick you but to make you think about what the purpose of the text you have just read was, i.e. why they were telling you about something. For example, was it aiming to help you find a part-time job or educate you about healthy eating?

## For the whole Reading paper:

- Complete all three texts in the same way.

- Watch your timing. All three texts are the same length so you should split up your time evenly.

- If you are stuck on one individual question, or find one complete Reading passage difficult, move on and go back at the end.

- Don't forget that you have the Writing question to do once you have finished the Reading questions.

## The Writing exam

For section 2 of the Reading and Writing paper you have to write an email of 120–150 words in French, applying for a job.

The Writing question is marked in a series of pegged marks. That means that there are set marks for different categories.

| | |
|---|---|
| Very good | 20 marks |
| Good | 16 marks |
| Satisfactory | 12 marks |
| Unsatisfactory | 8 marks |
| Poor | 4 marks |
| Very poor | 0 marks |

There is no set language that must be included in the Writing question to get the mark for each category – just broad guidelines as to what should be included.

The Writing question will be marked on three separate areas – **Content, Accuracy and Language**.

The first area that will probably be looked at is the **Content**. The person marking your Writing exam will read your answer to check that you have included information on all six bullet points that are listed in the question.

— The first four bullet points, which are the same each year, must be covered in detail and accurately. These are: personal information, school experience, skills/interests, work experience/jobs.

— For the two bullet points that are unpredictable, you must answer them fully. You do not need to go into a great deal of detail and you will get away with being less accurate, although if you make lots of mistakes or very serious mistakes this will affect your mark. Go for simple but accurate information.

— To get top marks all bullet points must be covered evenly. Don't write loads for the first two bullet points and then less for the others. It gives the impression that you do not know all the details needed and are running out of steam.

— To make sure that all six bullet points are covered evenly it is a good idea to plan your essay.

— Take 5 minutes or so to work out what you are going to write for each point and stick to the plan.

— The overall essay is 120–150 words so you should aim to write around 25–30 words in each section. This means writing probably only about two or three sentences for each point.

— You really should have an idea of what you will be writing for the first four bullet points before you go into the exam. You just need to make sure that you take the information you have worked on in class and make it relevant to the job advert in the exam.

— Use the plan to organise and make sure that you have not missed anything out. Sometimes people panic in an exam and they forget to put in information that is not only essential but they have already prepared. This can have an impact on your mark so take the time to sort out your essay before you start and keep referring to your plan as you are writing.

- Although you do not know the last two bullet points before the exam, they will be based on work that has been covered in class. Don't panic about these. Prepare sample answers in your plan.

- It is essential that you stick to verbs and vocabulary that you know for these last two bullet points. Don't rely on a dictionary. This may seem strange advice but this is when candidates start to write very poor quality French and this then has an effect on your final mark. Remember that you will only be writing a couple of sentences for each point so don't get carried away. The only time you should use a dictionary is to check spelling/gender, etc., not to plan complete sentences. The marker will be looking for accuracy and relevance. Don't show off unless you are sure of what you are writing.

Not only is it important to make sure you have the content correct, you must make sure that what you write is **Accurate**. This is the second area that will be looked at by the marker.

- If you have covered all the bullet points then the marker will look at the quality and accuracy of the verbs you use – the more accurate and varied, the better your grade. If you make a lot of mistakes with your verbs or use the same couple of verbs you will not get a good mark!

- Even if you make a few mistakes it will be possible to get 20/20 – very good. When looking at accuracy the marker will be looking at the quality of your language and how much in control of the language you are. A few spelling mistakes will be fine – any serious mistakes with verbs will mean that you will start to be penalised.

- As a rule of thumb, the better the quality of language you use, the less likely you are to be penalised for a few small errors.

If you cover all the bullet points and your verbs are accurate you have probably passed and the marker will then go on to look at other **Language** features you have used. This is the third area that will be looked at.

Language features you should include:

- adjectives

- adverbs

- time phrases – frequency

- prepositions

- conjunctions/linking words

- accurate spelling

Also:

- don't just stick to 'je' – use other personal pronouns ('on', 'il', etc.)

- avoid lists

# Example: answering bullet point 1

Look at this example of a paragraph regarding your school experience until now.

*Je vais à Newtown High school. Je suis en cinquième. Je vais passer six examens de National 5 en maths, histoire, anglais, chimie, français et musique. Je voudrais passer trois Highers et je voudrais aller à l'université.*

This would get you a satisfactory mark because it is mainly correct but very basic. Compare this to the sentences below, which tell you much the same thing.

*Je suis élève à Newtown High School. Je suis en cinquième donc je dois passer mes examens à la fin de l'année scolaire en juin. J'espère les réussir tous et bien sûr avec de bonnes notes parce que j'ai l'intention de continuer mes études au lycée l'année prochaine. Après avoir quitté l'école, je compte aller à l'université. J'aimerais aller à la fac à Édimbourg car je voudrais quitter la maison de mes parents et trouver un appartement avec des copains.*

This is still quite simple but is a better way of saying what school you go to.

This is a good conjunction to use to join the two parts of the sentence together.

'Je dois' + infinitive is a good structure to use. It is easy to use but sounds quite complex.

*Je suis élève à Newtown High School. Je suis en cinquième donc je dois passer mes examens à la fin de l'année scolaire en juin.*

This adds detail about when you will sit exams.

This phrase doesn't add to the meaning of the sentence but it makes it sound more natural and more French.

An adjective has been added.

This adds in a more detailed way of saying what you plan to do...

*J'espère les réussir tous et bien sûr avec de bonnes notes parce que j'ai l'intention de continuer mes études au lycée l'année prochaine.*

... and that you will stay on at school.

This is a good construction to use at National 5. 'Après avoir' + past participle is easy to learn but sounds complicated.

This varies from 'je pense' or 'je vais'. It is good to vary the verbs used.

This is another way to say to go to university. It is a shorter, more natural way. This shows you know both ways to say it.

*Après avoir quitté l'école, je compte aller à l'université. J'aimerais aller à la fac à Édimbourg car je voudrais quitter la maison de mes parents et trouver un appartement avec des copains.*

This adds extra information.

## Examples of structures

The following structures are designed to help you with all the bullet points but are only a guideline; there are many more structures you can use.

## Personal information

| | |
|---|---|
| Je voudrais poser ma candidature pour le poste de ………………..……….…..…….…… | I would like to apply for the position …………………………………………… **You need to start the email saying that you want to apply for the job. Read the advert carefully to make sure you apply for the correct job.** |
| Je m'appelle …………………………… | My name is …………………………………… |
| J'ai ……………………………… ans. | I am ………………………… years old. |
| J'habite à ……………………………… en Écosse. | I live in ……………… in Scotland. |
| …………………… est une grande/ petite ville dans le nord/sud/est/ouest de l'Écosse. | …………… is a big/small town in the north/south/east/west of Scotland. **There isn't much variety in what you say here – so make sure you don't make a simple mistake. Watch how you spell 'je m'appelle'. Make sure that you write your age as a word, not figures, and that you use 'ans' with age. You must put 'à' + town and 'en' + country (most countries) for where you live.** |
| J'habite à la campagne/en banlieue/dans un village. | I live in the country/in the suburbs/in a village. |
| J'aime mon quartier/mon village car il y a toujours quelque chose d'intéressant à faire ici et tous mes copains habitent près de chez moi. | I like my area/my village because there is always something interesting to do here and all my friends live near to me. |
| Je n'aime pas habiter ici car c'est trop tranquille et mes amis habitent loin de chez moi. | I don't like living here because it is too quiet and my friends live far away from my house. |

| | |
|---|---|
| Je suis + nationality<br>Je viens de + country<br>Ma famille vient de + country | I am + nationality<br>I come from + country<br>My family comes from + country<br><br>**The person marking will be able to see if you are male or female so get the masculine and feminine correct for nationality. This is good if you are not Scottish. You can say you live in Scotland but your nationality is different. You can then say where you or your family come from to explain this. Although it is not very complicated, it raises the quality of the French used.** |

**School experience**

| | |
|---|---|
| Je vais à + name of school. | I go to + name of school. |
| C'est un bon lycée. | It is a good school. |
| C'est un lycée + adjective to describe it – mixte, sympa, excellent | It is a mixed/nice/excellent school. |
| Cette année, j'étudie ........................ | This year I am studying ...................... |
| J'ai choisi d'étudier ........................ | I chose to study ............................... |
| Je suis obligé d'étudier ..................... | I have to study ................................ |
| | **Don't worry about putting all your subjects – a big list does not read well and although it won't lose you marks, it does not make a good impression.** |
| Ma matière préférée, c'est ...................... car | My favourite subject is ..................... because |
| • le prof est sympa | • the teacher is nice |
| • le prof nous aide beaucoup | • the teacher helps a lot |
| • je trouve que c'est une matière facile/intéressante | • I find it an easy/interesting subject |
| • je m'entends bien avec mon prof | • I get on well with my teacher |
| Je ne peux pas supporter ..................... car c'est très difficile/ennuyeux/ça ne m'intéresse pas du tout. | I can't stand ................... because it is very difficult/boring/it doesn't interest me at all. |

| | |
|---|---|
| La matière que je n'aime pas c'est …………………………………… | The subject that I don't like is …………… |
| Je m'intéresse beaucoup à ……… donc j'ai décidé de l'étudier cette année. | I am really interested in ………… so I have decided to study it this year. |
| | **The sentences below give extra information about school. Choose a couple of sentences like these to put in your essay.** |
| Au lycée je fais partie d'un club de ………………………………… | At school I am in a …………… club. |
| Heureusement, la plupart de élèves de mon école sont sympas et ils travaillent dur. | Luckily, most of the pupils at my school are nice and work hard. |
| Mon école a été rénovée il y a quelques années, et maintenant c'est plus grand et bien équipé. | My school was renovated several years ago and now it is bigger and well equipped. |
| Les cours commencent à neuf heures moins cinq et finissent vers trois heures dix, sauf le mercredi quand on a un cours de plus et qu' on qu'on finit à quatre heures. | Lessons start at five to nine and finish at ten past three except Wednesday when we have an extra lesson and finish at four o'clock. |
| Il est important d'étudier une langue étrangère parce que c'est très utile pour ma carrière. | It is important to study a foreign language because it is very useful for my career. |
| En ce qui me concerne, il y a trop de devoirs à faire le soir et le week-end. | For me there is too much homework to do in the evening and at the weekend. |
| À mon école on est obligé de porter l'uniforme. Pour moi, c'est insupportable. | At my school we have to wear uniform. I find it unbearable. |
| Je pense que l'uniforme n'est pas toujours très confortable. | I think that the uniform is not always very comfortable. |
| C'est une bonne idée car c'est moins cher. | It is a good idea because it is less expensive. |

**Skills/interests**

| | |
|---|---|
| Comme passe-temps j'aime + infinitive | As a hobby I like to ………………………… |
| Dans mes heures de loisirs j'aime + infinitive | In my free time I like to ………………… |

| | |
|---|---|
| Mon passe-temps préféré est + noun | My favourite hobby is .......................... |
| Pour me distraire, je préfère + infinitive | As a hobby I like ............................... |
| | **Mention a few hobbies** |
| Je suis membre de l'équipe scolaire de foot/natation. | I am a member of the school football/ swim team. |
| Je sais jouer de + musical instrument et je fais partie de l'orchestre de mon école. | I know how to play ........................ and I am in the school orchestra. |
| Je joue au tennis. | I play tennis. |
| | **Say when you do the hobby** |
| le week-end/le samedi après-midi/le vendredi soir/une fois par semaine/par mois/tous les jours/pendant les vacances/ en été/quand il pleut. | at the weekend/Saturday afternoon/Friday evening/once a week/month/every day/ during the holidays/in summer/when it rains. |
| | **Say where you do the hobby** |
| au centre de loisirs/à la piscine/chez moi/à l'école/au parc. | at the sports centre/at the pool/at my house/at school/in the park. |
| | **Finally, say what you think of it** |
| C'est amusant/je le trouve très intéressant/ c'est passionnant/ça me maintient en forme. | It is amusing/I find it very interesting/it is fascinating/it keeps me fit. |
| | **Try to use a sentence to link it to the job advert** |
| Mon passe-temps m'a montré l'importance de travailler en équipe et de travailler dur. | My hobby showed me the importance of working as a team and working hard. |
| Puisque j'ai joué dans l'équipe de foot, je peux travailler avec les autres. | As I play in the football team I can work with others. |
| Avec tous mes passe-temps et mes études, je suis très organisé(e). | With all my hobbies and my studies I am very organised. |

**Work experience/jobs**

| | |
|---|---|
| | **Write about work experience. Even if you have not done any – make it up. It is a good chance to use the perfect and imperfect tenses.** |
| J'ai déjà fait un stage dans un garage/un bureau/une école/un restaurant pendant une semaine/une quinzaine. | I did my work experience in a garage/office/ school/restaurant for a week/a fortnight. |

| | |
|---|---|
| J'ai travaillé comme ........................ | I worked as ........................... |
| Le patron était/mes collègues étaient + adjective | The boss/my colleagues were ............................................. |
| Tout le monde était très accueillant. | Everybody was very welcoming. |
| Tous les jours, je devais classer des documents/servir les clients/répondre au téléphone. | Every day, I had to file documents/serve customers/answer the phone. |
| Mon stage m'a beaucoup plu/c'était une bonne expérience. | I liked my work experience a lot/it was a good experience. |
| Je n'ai pas du tout aimé mon stage/c'était ennuyeux. | I did not like my work experience at all/it was boring. |
| | **It's also a good idea to talk about a part time job. Most students will not have a job, but you can make one up.** |
| Depuis le début de l'année, j'ai un petit boulot. | Since the start of the year I have had a part time job. |
| J'aime mon petit job. J'aime travailler avec les gens/travailler en plein air. | I like my job. I like to work with people/to work in the fresh air. |
| Je déteste mon job parce que je n'aime pas travailler avec les enfants/les journées sont longues et ennuyeuses. | I hate my job because I don't like to work with children/the days are long and boring. |
| Je travaille dans un café le samedi et le dimanche/je livre des journaux tous les matins/soirs/je fais du baby-sitting pour mes voisins le week-end. | I work in a café on Saturday and Sunday/I deliver papers every morning/evening/I babysit for my neighbours at the weekends. |
| Le travail est bien/mal payé. | The work is well/badly paid. |
| Je gagne 6€ de l'heure. Ce n'est pas beaucoup mais au moins cela me fait de l'argent de poche. | I earn 6 euros an hour. It's not a lot but at least I have my own money. |
| J'aime gagner de l'argent parce que je peux m'acheter ce que je veux/je voudrais aller en vacances avec mes copains. | I like to earn money because I am able to buy what I want/I would like to go on holiday with my friends. |

**Although the wording may be different, possible areas that could come up for the other two bullet points include:**

- **Request for information**

| | |
|---|---|
| Je voudrais demander des renseignements sur ce poste. | I would like to ask for information about this position. |
| Je dois travailler combien d'heures par jour? | How many hours do I have to work a day? |
| Je commence à quelle heure le matin? | At what time do I start in the morning? |
| On gagne combien de l'heure? | How much would I earn an hour? |
| En quoi constitue le travail? | What do I have to do in the job? |
| Est-ce qu'il faut porter un uniforme? | Do I have to wear a uniform? |

- **Reasons why you have applied for the job**

| | |
|---|---|
| Je voudrais poser ma candidature pour ce poste car ………………………………… | I would like to apply for this job because ………………………………………… |
| J'aime le contact avec les autres. | I like to meet other people. |
| J'adore parler le français. | I love speaking French. |
| Je voudrais continuer à étudier les langues. | I would like to continue to study languages. |
| J'aimerais améliorer mon français. | I would like to improve my French. |
| Je voudrais travailler à l'étranger. | I would like to work abroad. |
| J'aimerais travailler comme ………………………………………… | I would like to work as ………………………………………… |
| Je suis très énergique/honnête/sincère. | I am very energetic/honest/sincere. |

- **Describing a previous visit to France**

| | |
|---|---|
| Il y a deux ans/l'année dernière, je suis allé(e) en France avec ma famille/en groupe scolaire. | Two years ago/last year/I went to France with my family/on a school trip. |
| J'ai passé une semaine extraordinaire. | I had a great week. |
| On a visité beaucoup de monuments. C'était un peu ennuyeux. | We visited lots of monuments. It was a bit boring. |
| On était logé dans une famille française/dans une auberge de jeunesse/dans un hôtel. C'était génial. | We stayed with a French family/in a youth hostel/a hotel. It was great. |
| J'ai goûté les spécialités de la région. | I tasted the specialities of the region. |
| Je suis allé(e) dans une école française. C'était très différent, mais je préfère les écoles en Écosse. | I went to a French school. It was very different but I prefer school in Scotland. |

- **Previous experience you have that makes you suitable for the job**

**Look carefully at this bullet point. If it comes up, write about your work experience for bullet point 3 and write about a part-time job here (or vice versa).**

- **Your availability – when you can go for interview and start work**

| | |
|---|---|
| Est-ce que je dois passer un entretien d'embauche? | Do I have to come for a job interview? |
| Je peux venir passer un entretien d'embauche si c'est nécessaire. | I can come for an interview if necessary. |
| Je peux commencer le travail fin juin. | I can start at the end of June. |
| Je ne peux pas commencer à travailler avant la fin du mois de juin car je suis toujours à l'école. | I am not able to start work before the end of June as I am still at school. |
| Je peux travailler tout l'été. | I would be able to work all summer. |
| Je peux venir en France pour passer un entretien d'embauche si vous voulez. | I can travel to France for an interview if you want. |
| Je ne peux pas venir en France pour passer un entretien d'embauche. On peut discuter au téléphone ou sur Skype. | I can't travel to France for an interview. We could speak on the phone or via Skype. |

## Linking phrases

| | |
|---|---|
| heureusement | luckily/fortunately |
| malheureusement | unfortunately |
| cependant | however |
| donc | so/therefore |
| pourtant | however |
| c'est-à-dire | that is to say |
| en général | generally |
| néanmoins | nevertheless |
| surtout | above all |
| en plus | in addition |
| probablement | probably |
| de toute façon | anyway |

**It is a good idea to try to link together sentences in as many different ways as possible. The list here is just a few examples of words you could use. Don't overuse them but it will help your mark if you vary your sentence structure and don't just stick to simple sentences.**

## Marking guidance

This table gives you an idea of what is needed for a very good, a good and an unsatisfactory mark.

### Very good: 20

| How the question has been addressed | Mistakes made | Grammar and language features included |
| --- | --- | --- |
| • All points answered evenly, including the last two bullet points.<br>• Answers in sentences using a variety of structures. That means you need to use different verbs. You can't keep using the same structures. Where appropriate you should include different tenses.<br>• The overall application should be planned and logical and read well. | • Although it is important to be accurate, you can still get full marks with a few minor errors. The important thing is that the mistakes are not serious. This means that you can have one or two wrong spellings or 'la' where it should be 'le' but when you start making mistakes with verbs you will not get full marks.<br>• The more complex the language you use the more likely it is that a few small mistakes will be allowed. | • It is likely that each sentence will have a new verb and that a variety of tenses will be used. It is a good idea to use modal verbs – verbs like devoir, pouvoir.<br>• Care should be taken to include adjectives and to make sure that they are in the correct position and agree with the noun. It is a good idea to try to include unusual or irregular adjectives as well as making sure that you use some adverbs and prepositions.<br>• Sentences should be joined with a range of conjunctions. You can't just stick to 'et' (and) or 'puis' (then) – you need to have conjunctions like 'cependant' (however), 'puisque' (since), 'néanmoins' (nevertheless). |

## Good: 16

| | | |
|---|---|---|
| • All bullet points must be addressed but they do not have to be in as much detail, so can be a bit shorter and there can be a bit of repetition.<br>• In this category the writing is still accurate, just a bit simpler.<br>• All of the predicted bullet points must be addressed but one of the last two bullet points might not be completed at this level. | • Once again the verbs have to be correct.<br>• Often a piece of writing moves from 20 marks to 16 because of the amount of small errors there are with spelling, adjectives not agreeing, mistakes with accents (or missing them out).<br>• As with the category above, the more detailed your work is the more errors you can make.<br>• You will be likely to lose fewer marks by making mistakes in the last two bullet points as they are not known before the exam. | • There is less variety in the language used and the sentences are not so complex.<br>• The same verb can be used again (although there still has to be a reasonable range).<br>• Sentences would normally be shorter and so fewer conjunctions used. |

## Unsatisfactory: 8

| | | |
|---|---|---|
| • The bullet points are not fully covered. One or perhaps both of the last two bullet points might not be completed in this category.<br>• Sentences are less detailed and the language used is repetitive.<br>• For the job application to be in the unsatisfactory category there may be a part of it that the marker finds difficult to understand. | • The most common reasons for writing being placed in this unsatisfactory category are the mistakes with the verbs used, both in terms of spelling and mistakes with tenses.<br>• The errors in the writing cause confusion and make the meaning unclear. | • The sentences are basic and inaccurate. One or perhaps both of the last two bullet points might not be completed at this level.<br>• Verbs used are limited and inaccurate.<br>• The only accurate responses are for bullet points 1 and 2 about personal information.<br>• There are examples of mother tongue interference, i.e. English words occasionally appear in the job application. |

# The Listening exam

In the National 5 Listening exam you are not allowed to use a dictionary, so to do well you need to learn as much vocabulary as you can. Practise listening as often as possible.

There will be two listening passages. The first will involve one person speaking and is worth 8 marks. The second will be a conversation between two people, with one person asking questions of the other. This passage is worth 12 marks.

Here are some things you need to remember to get the best marks:

- Read over the questions. Use the vocabulary you have learned to help you predict what answers might come up.

- You will hear each section three times. The first time you hear the passage, just listen and think about the questions. It may be difficult to stop yourself, but do not write. If you start to write you may miss part of the next answer and this can lead to confusion.

- When the passage has finished, make notes.

- On the second listening, look at the questions and write notes to fill in all the points of the questions.

- On the third listening, fill in any gaps in your answers.

- You do not need to answer in as much detail as you do in the Reading section of the exam – but, remember, you do not have a dictionary, so you need to know a great deal of vocabulary.

- This is worth repeating – to do well you need to know your vocabulary. You cannot know too many words and the main focus of your study should be on learning as much vocabulary as you can.

## 'What is the purpose?' question

- The last question in the first passage will ask you the purpose of the first person's monologue.

- You will have to choose from three options and tick the box you think gives the correct answer.

- This question is not designed to trick you, but to make you think about the purpose of the passage, i.e. why was the person telling you about something. For example, to encourage you to visit a particular country or to persuade you to eat healthy foods.

When you have answered all the questions as well as you can:

- Read over your answers to make sure they make sense.

- Check all your answers are in English. Any French (even if it is the correct answer) will not get any marks.

# Practice paper A

FRENCH
NATIONAL 5
**Paper A**
**Reading and Writing**

You are given 1 hour and 30 minutes to finish this paper.

Total marks: 50

**Section 1: Reading (30 marks)**

Read the three texts and try to answer all of the questions.

Remember to answer in English.

**Section 2: Writing (20 marks)**

You can use a French dictionary for both the Reading and the Writing exams.

# Section 1: Reading (30 marks)

## Text 1

While in France you read an article about a young person and his problems with the internet.

Aujourd'hui la plupart des gens ont accès à l'Internet très facilement – sur leur ordinateur ou sur leur téléphone portable. Mais certains pensent que ce n'est pas une bonne idée parce qu'on a créé une génération accro à l'Internet et les jeux vidéo. Ça veut dire qu'ils sont dépendants.

Claude – 21 ans, chef cuisinier à Paris: «Il y a deux ans, j'avais un vrai problème avec les jeux vidéo. Je faisais des longues journées et je travaillais très dur au restaurant et c'était épuisant. Normalement, à la fin de la journée, on rentre chez soi tout de suite et on va au lit car on est crevé. Mais quand je rentrais à la maison, je ne me couchais pas. Dès que je rentrais dans mon appartement, j'allais sur l'ordinateur et je ne bougeais pas pendant toute la nuit car je jouais sur Internet. Le lendemain, j'étais très fatigué au restaurant et j'avais des difficultés à faire mon travail correctement. En plus, je ne sortais jamais avec mes copains et je ne voyais plus ma famille.

Tout a changé quand mon patron m'a presque renvoyé. Je me suis aperçu que mon boulot était plus important que les jeux vidéo et je me suis arrêté tout de suite.»

## Questions

**a.** Why do people think that it is not a good idea to have easy access to the Internet?

_____

_____

1

**b.** What does Claude say about his days at work? Complete the sentence.

I worked long days and worked _____ at the restaurant and it was _____

**2**

**c.** What should you normally do when you finish work?

_____

_____

**2**

**d.** What did Claude do as soon as he came home? Give two examples.

_____

_____

**2**

**e.** How did this affect his work?

_____

_____

**2**

**f.** When did things change? Give one example.

_____

_____

**1**

## Text 2

You then read this article about differences between school in France and in Scotland.

En Écosse, si on ne travaille pas à l'école, on risque d'avoir de mauvaises notes et des ennuis à la maison si les parents sont fâchés. En France, si on ne réussit pas à l'école, on risque le redoublement. Cela signifie que, à la rentrée, en septembre, on se retrouve dans une classe au même niveau que l'année précédente.

Imaginez la honte et la colère des parents si en juin leur enfant reçoit un bulletin scolaire sur lequel il est écrit qu'il est obligé de redoubler l'année scolaire. Le redoublement est officiellement présenté comme une chance supplémentaire, mais en réalité pour tout le monde cela représente une année ratée à l'école.

À seize ans, en France, on peut quitter l'école mais comme en Écosse beaucoup d'élèves continuent leurs études car ils veulent passer leur bac. À cause du redoublement, il y a des élèves de dix-neuf ou même vingt ans qui sont toujours au lycée.

En France, certains sont contre le redoublement, mais la plupart des gens pensent que c'est une bonne idée car cela incite les jeunes à travailler et surtout à réussir leurs examens.

## Questions

**a.** What happens in Scotland if you don't work at school?

2

_____

_____

**b.** In France, what happens if you don't work at school?

_____

_____

**1**

**c.** Complete the sentence using the information in the passage.

Imagine the _____ and _____ of the parents if in June their

child receives _____ saying that they have to repeat a year.

**3**

**d.** How is repeating a year officially explained?

_____

_____

**1**

**e.** What does repeating a year mean to everybody?

_____

_____

**1**

**f.** Why do most of the population think having the risk of repeating a year is a good idea?

_____

_____

**2**

## Text 3

You then read this article about jobs.

---

### Comment trouver un petit boulot?

- Tout d'abord, il faut préparer un CV contenant tous les détails nécessaires. Par exemple, les détails personnels – ton nom, ton adresse, ton âge, mais aussi tes qualifications et les examens que tu vas passer. Le plus important, c'est la partie où tu décris tes intérêts, ce que tu aimes faire pendant ton temps libre. En lisant cela, un employeur peut savoir ce que tu aimes faire et cela va l'aider à décider si tu es le genre de personne qu'il veut employer.

- Puis tu dois envoyer le CV à tous les entreprises, les magasins et les restaurants de ton quartier, mais il ne faut pas s'arrêter là. C'est une bonne idée de confirmer l'envoi de ton CV par un coup de téléphone et de persévérer. Cependant, pour trouver un petit boulot, le mieux c'est d'aller demander en personne dans les magasins ou les restaurants puisque c'est comme ça que les petites entreprises trouvent leurs employés.

- Enfin, il faut penser à tous les genres de petits boulots que tu peux trouver près de chez toi. Peut-être que tes voisins ont besoin d'un coup de main dans leur jardin. Y a-t-il des personnes de ta famille qui voudraient payer quelqu'un pour faire le ménage? Si tu aimes les enfants, tu pourrais passer une petite annonce pour voir s'il y a des familles dans le quartier qui ont besoin de quelqu'un pour garder leurs enfants.

---

### Questions

**a.** What is the most important part of a CV?

1

_____

_____

**b.** Why is that important to an employer?

_____

_____

1

**c.** What should you do with your CV?

_____

_____

1

**d.** You should not stop there. What should you do?

_____

_____

1

**e.** What is the best way to find a job and why?

_____

_____

2

**f.** What kinds of jobs could you look for? Tick three box.

| | |
|---|---|
| Do the garden for your neighbours | |
| Clean your neighbour's car | |
| Do housework for your relatives | |
| Do your neighbour's housework | |
| Advertise to wash cars | |
| Babysitting | |

3

**g.** What is the article aimed at doing? Tick one box.

| | |
|---|---|
| Helping you find a job | |
| Telling you what type of job is best | |
| Getting you to take a job working for your neighbours | |

1

# Section 2: Writing (20 marks)

You see this job advertised and you decide to send an email to the company to apply for the post.

---

Hôtel du Parc à Lyon recherche un/une réceptionniste.

Vous devez avoir une excellente présentation, aimer le contact avec les autres et parler plusieurs langues étrangères.

Pour plus de détails ou si ce poste vous intéresse, contactez M. Martin à l'adresse électronique suivante: mmartinhotel@google.fr

---

When you prepare your application email, you must make sure that you include information from all of the following points:

- Personal information (name, age, where you live).

- Information about what you have experienced at school or college to the present day.

- Any skills/interests you have that make you the best candidate for the job.

- What work experience you have that would be relevant to the job you are applying for.

- Questions about what your duties will be and what your hours will be.

- Some details about a previous trip to France you have already made.

The email should be around 120–150 words long. You may use a French dictionary.

The Listening exam should take approximately 25 minutes.

Total marks: 20

You will hear two passages in French. You will have 1 minute to study the questions before you hear each passage.

The two passages are each repeated three times. There will be a pause of 1 minute between each repetition.

There will be a pause in which you can write your answers after each passage.

Remember to answer in English and write your answers in the spaces provided.

You are allowed to make notes as you listen but can only write on the exam paper.

You cannot use a French dictionary.

## Passage 1

Claire is talking about where she is living at the moment.

**a.** Why is she living in Senegal just now?

_____

_____

**1**

**b.** What is different about school?

_____

_____

**1**

**c.** **(i)** Why is their balcony so useful? Give one example.

_____

_____

**1**

**(ii)** Why are they able to use it most of the year? Give one example.

_____

_____

**1**

**d.** What has Claire bought at the market? Complete the sentence.

At the market she bought _____ _____and _____

**2**

**e.** What has she noticed that there is not a lot of at the market?

_____

_____

**f.** Why is Claire talking about this? Tick one box.

| | |
|---|---|
| To tell you about her life in Dakar | |
| To tell you about her life in France | |
| To tell you about what you can do in Dakar | |

MARKS
Do not write in this margin

## Passage 2

Julie asks her friend Guy about his holiday last year.

**a.** Why did Guy go to Quebec on holiday? Give two examples.

2

_____

_____

**b.** What did he do for the first week of his holiday? Give two examples.

2

_____

_____

**c.** What types of food did he try? Give three examples.

3

_____

_____

**d.** Where did he go in the second week? Tick one box.

1

| | |
|---|---|
| His uncle took him to the lake by car | |
| His uncle took him to the mountains by car | |
| His uncle took him to visit his aunt by car | |

**e.** What did he say about the journey? Give one example.

1

_____

_____

**f.** What new thing did he try there?

1

_____

_____

**g. (i)** What did he like most about his holiday?

**1**

_____

_____

**(ii)** Why?

**1**

_____

_____

9. (i) What did he like most about his holiday?

_____

_____

(ii) Why?

_____

_____

FRENCH

NATIONAL 5

**Paper A**

**Listening transcript**

The listening transcripts accompany the audio tracks, which can be downloaded, free, from the Leckie website at https://collins.co.uk/pages/scottish-curriculum-free-resources-french

Remember that listening transcripts will NOT be provided when you sit your final exam. They are printed here as an additional item to help you with your revision for the Listening exam.

the education publisher
**for Scotland**

## Listening Transcript: Passage 1

Claire is talking about where she is living at the moment.

Bonjour. Je m'appelle Claire. Je suis française mais en ce moment j'habite au Sénégal puisque mon père va travailler pendant un an dans le bureau de Dakar de l'entreprise pour laquelle il travaille. Dakar est la plus grande ville et aussi la capitale du pays.

Ma vie ici n'est pas si différente de ma vie en France. Je vais à une école au centre de la ville. Au lycée, j'étudie les mêmes matières et le règlement de l'école est presque le même que celui de mon école en France. Ce qui est différent au Sénégal pour moi, c'est qu'on est obligé de porter un uniforme scolaire.

Notre appartement se trouve dans un grand immeuble. On a un très grand balcon qu'on utilise comme salle de séjour et salle à manger. Le climat est très doux et il fait si chaud qu'on peut manger dehors sur le balcon toute l'année.

Comme en France, je vais souvent au marché avec mes parents et avec mes amis. Ici on peut acheter de tout – des fruits, des plantes et des animaux. Il y a aussi une grande variété de bracelets et de boucles d'oreilles. J'ai déjà acheté quelques T-shirts et un sac à main. J'ai remarqué qu'il n'y a pas beaucoup de chaussures au marché.

Ma famille et moi, nous devrons rentrer en France bientôt et je garderai de bons souvenirs de mon année à Dakar et je suis sûre que les couleurs vives du marché resteront mon meilleur souvenir.

## Listening Transcript: Passage 2

Julie asks her friend Guy about his holiday last year.

### Où es-tu allé en vacances l'année dernière?

L'année dernière, je suis allé au Québec au Canada. J'ai de la famille là-bas. Ma mère est née au Canada et j'ai voulu rendre visite à mes tantes et cousins qui habitent là-bas. C'était des vacances différentes et ça m'a fait très plaisir de voir ma famille. J'ai séjourné chez une tante et je suis allé voir mes oncles et mes cousins qui habitent dans le même quartier.

### Qu'est-ce que tu as fait pendant ton séjour?

La première semaine, je suis resté dans la ville de Montréal, la ville principale de la région. C'est une ville historique et c'est très pittoresque. Il y a aussi beaucoup de choses à faire. J'ai adoré la vieille ville. J'ai passé un après-midi à faire les petits magasins dans les rues historiques. J'ai aussi visité les monuments intéressants dans la ville et le vieux port.

### As-tu goûté la cuisine de la région ?

On est allé au restaurant plusieurs fois. En général j'ai mangé la cuisine française mais je suis allé aussi dans un restaurant chinois. Ce que j'ai préféré c'était de déjeuner au café. Les petits snacks au café étaient savoureux.

### Et la deuxième semaine, qu'est-ce que tu as fait ?

La deuxième semaine, mon oncle nous a emmenés à la montagne en voiture. On a fait un long voyage. Le voyage a duré deux heures, mais le paysage était impressionnant. On a séjourné dans le chalet de ma tante. Je sais déjà faire du ski mais j'ai essayé de faire du snowboard pour la première fois. C'était tout à fait différent du ski mais cela m'a plu.

### Qu'est-ce que tu as préféré pendant tes vacances ?

Pour moi ce que j'ai préféré c'était quand je suis allé à un match de hockey sur glace. Mes cousins sont passionnés par le hockey. Ils y jouent et ils adorent regarder les matchs aussi. C'était animé et très bruyant mais j'ai trouvé ça génial.

# Practice paper B

# Practice Papers for SQA Exams

FRENCH

NATIONAL 5

**Paper B**

**Reading and Writing**

You are given 1 hour and 30 minutes to finish this paper.

Total marks: 50

## Section 1: Reading (30 marks)

Read the three texts and try to answer all of the questions.

Remember to answer in English.

## Section 2: Writing (20 marks)

You can use a French dictionary for both the Reading and the Writing exams.

Leckie

the education publisher

**for Scotland**

# Section 1: Reading (30 marks)

## Text 1

While you are in France you look at your French friend's school magazine where a pupil – Julie – gives her experiences of life in school.

Je suis en terminale au lycée en France et à la fin de l'année scolaire, je vais passer mes examens. Pendant toute ma scolarité, j'ai été une élève modèle. J'ai toujours fait mes devoirs quand il le fallait, jamais en retard, et j'ai bien préparé mes contrôles. D'habitude, j'avais de bonnes notes.

Cette année, j'ai continué à travailler. Mais tout est different, ce n'est pas si facile qu'avant. J'ai trouvé le travail en classe difficile à comprendre et je n'ai pas toujours très bien réussi. Heureusement, j'ai déjà passé mon examen de français l'année dernière, mais maintenant, au lieu des cours de français, il faut suivre des cours de philosophie. Ce n'est pas marrant!

Comme la plupart de mes amis, j'ai déjà commencé à préparer mon baccalauréat, que je passerai en juin, mais je m'inquiète pour les résultats. Je voudrais continuer mes études à la fac mais pour cela, je dois réussir tous mes examens et avec de bonnes notes.

Je rêve de l'été prochain. Plus d'études et plus de stress. Des semaines libres pour m'amuser et sortir avec des amis.

## Questions

**a.** How was Julie a model pupil?

2

_____

_____

MARKS
Do not write in this margin

**b.** This year, what is different from previous years at school? Give two examples. 2

**c.** Why doesn't she study French anymore? Tick one box. 1

| | |
|---|---|
| She sat the exam at the end of last year | |
| She didn't pick it | |
| She wasn't allowed to sit it | |

**d.** What happens instead? 1

**e.** Why is she worried? 1

**f.** What does she have to do to continue her studies? 1

**g.** What is she dreaming of and why? Give two examples. 2

## Text 2

You then read about a pupil from the school's exchange partner school in Scotland who has written about her holidays in France.

L'année dernière, je suis allée en France pendant quinze jours. D'habitude, je vais en France pendant les vacances car j'ai de la famille qui habite là-bas. Normalement, j'y vais en août, mais cette année, ma famille et moi n'avons pas pu y aller car mon père devait travailler, donc on est parti début juillet. On a trouvé les vacances en juillet beaucoup plus agréables.

D'abord, à cette période-là, c'est beaucoup plus tranquille et calme. Bien sûr, il y a des touristes comme nous, mais la plupart des Français travaillent encore, donc il n'y a que des vacanciers. En août, il y a du monde partout.

L'une des meilleures choses c'était les festivités du Quatorze Juillet. C'est la fête nationale en France et il y a des célébrations partout dans le pays. Dans le village où je passe mes vacances, pendant la journée, il y avait un grand marché et une foire le 14 juillet. Le soir, on a organisé un grand bal et un feu d'artifice. On a dansé, on a mangé et on s'est amusé.

L'année prochaine, on va retourner en France comme d'habitude et je vais persuader mes parents de partir à nouveau en juillet.

## Questions

**a.** Why did she not go on holiday in August as normal?

1

_____

_____

**b.** Why was it quieter than usual?

_____

_____

2

**c.** What did they think of the celebrations for the 14th July?

_____

_____

1

**d.** What do they do to celebrate in the village during the day?

_____

_____

2

**e.** What activities were there in the evening? Tick two boxes.

| | |
|---|---|
| There was a dance | |
| There were fireworks | |
| They had a bonfire | |
| They had a barbecue | |
| They played football | |

2

**f.** What is going to happen about next year's holiday?

_____

_____

2

## Text 3

You then read this article from Pierre explaining about his lifestyle.

Pour moi, vivre sainement, c'est très important. Il y a quatre ans, j'étais très malade. Ça m'inquiétait beaucoup et pour cette raison je fais très attention à ce que je mange, et surtout à la qualité de la nourriture que j'achète.

Bien sûr, c'est important pour moi de garder la ligne, mais le plus important c'est de me tenir en bonne santé. Pour être en pleine forme, je fais de l'exercice plusieurs fois par semaine. D'habitude, au centre sportif, je fais de l'aérobic, mais aussi quelquefois de la natation et chez moi j'ai un vélo d'appartement et j'essaie d'en faire quand je ne peux pas aller à la gym.

Quant à la nourriture, je fais des efforts pour suivre un régime équilibré. Je mange au moins cinq portions de fruits et légumes par jour, mais je prépare aussi des repas variés et nourrissants et, bien sûr, sains. Comme ça, je reste en bonne santé.

Je ne mange jamais de fast-food. Je trouve cette nourriture mauvaise pour la santé et de toute façon, j'ai l'habitude de manger de la nourriture fraîche et simple et je n'aime ni le goût ni l'odeur de ce qu'on mange dans les fast-foods.

## Questions

**a.** Why is it important for Pierre to eat healthily? Give two examples.

2

_____

_____

**b.** What does he do to keep fit?

3

| At the sports centre | |
|---|---|
| At home | |

**c.** What type of meals does he prepare?

2

_____

_____

**d.** Why does he not like fast food?

2

_____

_____

**e.** Why has Pierre written this article? Tick one box.

1

| To warn you about eating an unhealthy diet | |
|---|---|
| To tell you to do more exercise | |
| To explain why it is important to him that he eats healthily | |

# Section 2: Writing (20 marks)

You see this job advertised and you decide to send an email to the café to apply for the post.

---

Café de la gare recherche serveur/serveuse.

Vous devez avoir le sens des responsabilités et être ouvert. Vous devez parler le français, l'anglais et une autre langue étrangère.

Pour plus de renseignements, contactez M. Dupont à l'adresse électronique suivante: mdupontcafel@google.fr

---

When you prepare your application email you must make sure that you include information from all of the following points:

- Personal information (name, age, where you live).

- Information about what you have experienced at school or college to the present day.

- Any skills/interests you have which make you the best candidate for the job.

- What work experience you have that would be relevant to the job you are applying for.

- Ask if accommodation is provided.

- Tell them about a school trip you have made to Paris.

The email should be around 120–150 words long. You may use a French dictionary.

FRENCH
NATIONAL 5
**Paper B**
**Listening**

The Listening exam should take approximately 25 minutes.

Total marks: 20

You will hear two passages in French. You will have 1 minute to study the questions before you hear each passage.

The two passages are each repeated three times. There will be a pause of 1 minute between each repetition.

There will be a pause in which you can write your answers after each passage.

Remember to answer in English and write your answers in the spaces provided.

You are allowed to make notes as you listen but can only write on the exam paper.

You cannot use a French dictionary.

the education publisher
**for Scotland**

## Passage 1

When in France you talk to Françoise about finding a job.

**a.** What is Françoise having to do to help her find a job?

_____

_____

**b.** What are the easy details to fill in? Give two examples.

_____

_____

**c.** What hobbies does she have?

_____

_____

**d.** What is the problem about filling in information about her ambitions?

Give one example.

_____

_____

**e.** Where is she going to send her CV?

1

_____

_____

**f.** What is Françoise mainly telling you about? Tick one box.

1

| | |
|---|---|
| How to find a part time job | |
| Her search for a part time job | |
| What she wants to do in life | |

# Passage 2

You then listen to a conversation between Pierre and his friend Philippe about his search for a job.

**a.** Why is he looking for a part time job? Give two examples.

_____

_____

**2**

**b.** What is important for him in a part time job?

_____

_____

**2**

**c.** Where is Pierre going to look for a job?

_____

_____

**2**

**d.** What hours would he like to work? Fill in the table.

**2**

| During the summer | |
| When school goes back | |

**e.** What is Pierre going to do with the money he earns?

_____

_____

**2**

**f.** What does Pierre want to work as later on? Give two examples.

_____

_____

**2**

# N5 Practice Papers for SQA Exams

FRENCH
NATIONAL 5
**Paper B**
**Listening transcript**

The listening transcripts accompany the audio tracks, which can be downloaded, free, from the Leckie website at https://collins.co.uk/pages/scottish-curriculum-free-resources-french

Remember that listening transcripts will NOT be provided when you sit your final exam. They are printed here as an additional item to help you with your revision for the Listening exam.

⟨Leckie
the education publisher
**for Scotland**

**Listening Transcript: Passage 1**

When in France you talk to Françoise about finding a job.

Je cherche un petit boulot en ce moment et pour ça je dois préparer mon CV. Au début, je croyais que ça serait très facile, mais maintenant que j'essaie de le faire, j'ai quelques difficultés.

Pour les informations personnelles, c'est facile. Ce n'est pas compliqué d'écrire son adresse et sa date de naissance. C'est également facile de noter ses résultats aux examens. J'ai tous les certificats. Les difficultés commencent quand je dois écrire ce que je fais pendant mon temps libre et c'est encore plus dur quand je dois parler de mes ambitions.

Bien sûr, je fais beaucoup de choses pendant mes heures de loisirs. Je vais à la piscine plusieurs fois par semaine, je fais même partie d'un club de natation – mais je n'ai jamais rien gagné. J'adore jouer aux échecs, mais chez moi avec mon père ou ma sœur. Je ne participe jamais aux tournois.

Quant à mes ambitions, il y a un problème. Je n'ai aucune idée de ce que je voudrais faire dans ma vie. Pour l'instant, je suis toujours au lycée et je pense rarement à l'avenir.

Puisque c'est nécessaire pour moi de trouver un petit boulot, je vais finir mon CV. Je voudrais envoyer mon CV aux restaurants et aux magasins de ma ville le plus tôt possible.

## Listening Transcript: Passage 2

You then listen to a conversation between Pierre and his friend Philippe about his search for a job.

**Pierre, tu cherches un petit boulot en ce moment?**

Oui, maintenant que j'ai fini mes examens, je ne suis pas obligé d'étudier tous les week-ends et j'ai besoin d'un peu d'argent de poche pour financer mes loisirs.

**Qu'est-ce que tu voudrais faire comme boulot?**

Le plus important pour moi, c'est de trouver un emploi pas loin de chez moi et j'aimerais surtout travailler les week-ends plutôt que de travailler le soir.

**Tu as déjà essayé de trouver un emploi?**

Non, je vais commencer mes recherches ce week-end.

**Tu vas chercher où?**

D'abord, je vais me renseigner dans les cafés et les restaurants de la ville pour voir si je pourrais trouver un poste comme serveur.

Puis il y a quelques petits magasins dans le quartier historique. Je vais demander s'ils ont besoin d'un vendeur.

**Tu voudrais travailler combien d'heures par semaine?**

J'aimerais travailler à plein-temps pendant l'été, et si c'est possible, je voudrais travailler à mi-temps – le week-end ou après l'école après la rentrée en septembre.

**Qu'est-ce que tu penses faire de ton argent**

Je vais le dépenser un peu. Je voudrais m'acheter des vêtements et je devrais mettre un peu de côté pour mes vacances de ski en février.

**Qu'est-ce que tu voudrais faire comme métier dans la vie?**

Je ne sais pas encore. Je vais aller à la fac pour faire des études d'anglais et d'espagnol, et après, je vais travailler à l'étranger, peut-être en Amérique du Sud.